Praise for *Noor*

'Akbar Ahmed sets the clock ticking from the first moments of his wondrous new play, *Noor*. The three sons of Assad Hussein must find a way to get their beloved sister released from a US-sponsored prison, ironically referred to as the "Holiday Inn", before her honour is ruined. Dr Ahmed writes the voice of each of these sons – one a pacifist scholar, another a radicalised doctor, and another a timid, Westernised government official – with compassion and deep understanding. The great achievement of this spectacular play ... [is] characters whose universality is clear, while at the same time being living, breathing, grieving, struggling people with individual voices captured in utter specificity. Listen in rapture to the voices of modern Islam. I am in awe of this tremendous, important work.'

Daniel Futterman
Actor (Daniel Pearl in *A Mighty Heart*)
Academy Award-nominated screenwriter for *Capote*

Praise for *The Trial of Dara Shikoh*

'Professor Akbar Ahmed's brilliant new play, *The Trial of Dara Shikoh*, is not only a fascinating drama but a most important, highly instructive study of the major forces within Islam that continue to reflect the fatal struggle between Dara Shikoh and Aurangzeb that grip our modern world and may help to decide our global future.'

Stanley Wolpert
Professor Emeritus, University of California, Los Angeles

Akbar Ahmed

Akbar Ahmed: Two Plays

Introduction by

Ari Roth

Viva Books

New Delhi | Mumbai | Chennai | Kolkata | Bangalore | Hyderabad | Kochi | Guwahati

First Indian Edition 2010

VIVA BOOKS PRIVATE LIMITED

- 4737/23 Ansari Road, Daryaganj, New Delhi 110 002
  E-mail: vivadelhi@vivagroupindia.net, Tel. 42242200
- 76, Service Industries, Shirvane, Sector 1, Nerul, Navi Mumbai 400 706
  E-mail: vivamumbai@vivagroupindia.net, Tel. 27721273, 27721274
- Jamals Fazal Chambers, 26 Greams Road, Chennai 600 006
  E-mail: vivachennai@vivagroupindia.net, Tel. 28290304, 28294241
- B-103, Jindal Towers, 21/1A/3 Darga Road, Kolkata 700 017
  E-mail: vivakolkata@vivagroupindia.net, Tel. 22836381, 22816713
- 7, Sovereign Park Apartments, 56-58, K. R. Road, Basavanagudi, Bangalore 560 004
  E-mail: vivabangalore@vivagroupindia.net, Tel. 26607409, 26607410
- 101-102 Mughal Marc Apartments, 3-4-637 to 641, Narayanguda, Hyderabad 500 029
  E-mail: vivahyderabad@vivagroupindia.net, Tel. 27564481, 27564482
- First Floor, Beevi Towers, SRM Road, Kaloor, Kochi 682 018, Kerala
  E-mail: vivakochi@vivagroupindia.net, Tel: 0484-2403055, 2403056
- 232, GNB Road, Beside UCO Bank, Silpukhuri, Guwahati 781 003
  E-mail: vivaguwahati@vivagroupindia.net, Tel: 0361-2666386

www.vivagroupindia.com

Published by arrangement with
Westbourne Publishers Limited t/a Saqi
26 Westbourne Grove,
London W2 5RH
UK

ISBN 978-81-309-1395-7

Published by Vinod Vasishtha for Viva Books Private Limited, 4737/23, Ansari Road, Daryaganj, New Delhi - 110 002.

Printed and bound by Raj Press, R-3, Inderpuri, New Delhi - 110 012.

Contents

Introduction

It began with a stack of paper napkins, so the story goes, on a plane bound from Kansas to the nation's capital. Akbar Ahmed's flight was taxiing slowly, or maybe it was delayed. Either way, an idea had sprung, fully formed, into the globetrotting anthropologist's mind, and he just had to write his brainstorm down: a play about the crisis of modern Islam at an existential crossroads, calling to mind in form and function Ariel Dorfman's modern classic *Death and the Maiden*, a kidnapping drama about revenge enacted by a surviving torture victim. As the writing flowed, Dr Ahmed requested more napkins. Feverishly, he continued, full streams of dialogue punctuated by plot point after plot point, until a play had been committed to cocktail tissue. The stack of napkins numbered thirty tall (again, so the story goes; but the image of a play so urgently ushered forth into the world stays vividly in the mind, apocryphal or not). Soon would come the tasks of transcribing, revising, refining, workshopping and, finally, staging the play, the title of which came to Dr Ahmed at first conception: Noor. The word means 'light', which has been his charge as an educator from the very beginning: to spread the luminosity of understanding where darkness and ignorance have prevailed for too long.

I was one of the first recipients of this play, Dr Ahmed's first. We had met at a roundtable discussion of the very same *Death and the Maiden* at Washington's Theater J, a progressive Jewish theatre where an Islamic scholar like Akbar Ahmed would be warmly welcomed and closely listened to. It was Ramadan, and Dr Ahmed was fasting while taking in a matinee performance. We broke the fast collectively and symbolically by passing out dates and raisins to the post-show audience, and Dr Ahmed responded appreciatively to both the drama onstage and to the intercultural outreach that characterised the theatre's programming. Dr Ahmed was at home in this setting, public discourse following a cultural offering being second nature to this public-minded intellectual who could count among his notable career achievements the professional credits of 'published poet' and 'film producer'. But it would prove quite the challenge for the scholar to navigate the collaborative shoals of new play development on his way to becoming a produced playwright. For with *Noor* in the in-box at Theater J, Dr Ahmed had submitted his script to a dramaturgical school of tough love. Working in close collaboration with a supportive yet demanding team, including Theater J's literary director Shirley Serotsky who would stage the workshops, each line of dialogue and every stage direction in *Noor* would be pulled apart, questioned and massaged. The play would go through twelve drafts before fully emerging as a vigorously argued, powerfully dramatised work, fulfilling Dr Ahmed's most fundamental ambitions for it.

Noor is a tightly focused work about three Muslim brothers and their missing sister, and also a grand debate about the proverbial 'clash of civilisations' argued from the Eastern side of the divide. Through the power of its drama, it argues – as Dr Ahmed has argued throughout his distinguished career – that we must move from the paradigm of a 'clash' to a more sensitive conversation between kindred entities. The play speaks of fierce resentment and fervent zeal, but also counsels more tolerant acceptance. *Noor* begins with an act of brutality and continues to reveal several more: an offstage kidnapping in broad daylight by an unidentified paramilitary outfit; a home ransacked by investigating soldiers; a fundamentalist revenge plot; and a subsequent assassination proposed as an act of reprisal. The play also paints a grisly portrait of the kind of humiliation suffered by people held in captivity by thuggish and criminal representatives of a state or insurgency.

For all its mastery in describing desperate, violent scenes, informed no doubt by his experience in the field and as a Pakistani high commissioner and public servant, Dr Ahmed's play is simultaneously interlaced with evocations of grace and beauty: the poetry of Rumi, the transcendent spirit of Sufism, the rituals of eating that bind family members to their religious traditions and to each other. The play is also fully in touch with the socioeconomic and political realities of the modern world. It brilliantly places the brothers, each of whom represents a different strain of Islamic thought and practice, into an intellectual tug-of-war where, very much as in *Hamlet*, the question of what to do and how to respond to a grievous breach of family honour triggers a collective crisis of identity, revealing realms of insight into the condition of modern Islam in today's world.

In *The Trial of Dara Shikoh*, Dr Ahmed's follow-up to *Noor*, we are led back four centuries to the final days of a wise Mughal prince whose trial serves as an effective forum in which to assess the struggle between a liberal, humane Islam placed in opposition to the rigid intellectualism of a more orthodox and dominant Islamic theology. This three-act play is about the clash of two brothers who oppose each other because of their dramatic differences in temperament and world-views. Events in the play are based in history but constructed loosely for dramatic purposes. The brothers are also fighting for the throne of one of the most powerful and richest domains on earth, the Mughal Empire. At its peak, the Empire included what are now Afghanistan, Pakistan, India and Bangladesh.

Dr Ahmed teaches us much we never knew in this play of virtuosic historical story telling. We learn of an earlier Akbar, Akbar the Great, who ruled his empire in the 16th century through religious tolerance combined with sheer military might. His was probably the mightiest army the region had ever seen, including 50,000 steel-plated, armoured elephants which were the equivalent of our modern tanks. By the time Akbar the Great's grandson, the Emperor Shah Jehan was in power, the Mughal Empire was the richest in the world, with a population of about 130 million.

The Emperor had declared Dara Shikoh, his eldest son, his heir apparent. Dara was an extraordinary prince, both noble and bold in behaviour, but also a learned scholar of mysticism. Loved by mystics and sages alike, expectations ran high that India would finally have an emperor who could unite the different faiths and peoples of the land. Dara's younger brother Aurangzeb, an orthodox Muslim and a battle-hardened veteran, resented this declaration of succession. Many powerful Muslim nobles and generals preferred Aurangzeb in order to underline the Islamic nature of the Mughal Empire.

In Dr Ahmed's dramatic treatment, the trial and death of Dara Shikoh raises the big question, 'what if?' about India and the directions it could have taken had Dara succeeded to the Mughal throne. Dara's downfall is more than the death of a noble prince; it is also the rejection of a certain interpretation of Islam and attitude to the divine and politics here on earth.

Dr Ahmed's second play is more of a spectacle than the first, splashed with theatrical colour and ritual. It emerged even more fully formed from his pen than had *Noor*. It benefited from a glorious staging at the Katzen Arts Center of Washington's American University, including thoroughly committed performances from some of the area's leading South Asian actors.

Dr Ahmed, who is Ibn Khaldun Chair of Islamic Studies at the American University and Chair of Middle East and Islamic Studies at the US Naval Academy in Annapolis, Maryland, has written plays that examine both history and the present, offering lenses through which we can better understand predicaments and tensions in Muslim society. It's a great service to make these unique theatrical journeys available to audiences from all walks of life, and we are privileged to have as our guide a leading scholar of Islam and perhaps the only Pakistani playwright in the United States. Invariably, when these plays are presented – either as readings or full productions – houses sell out; people young and old, Muslim and non-Muslim, come from all over to attend; and the mainstream press pays attention. Akbar Ahmed is a rare blend of scholar, popular lecturer, poet, playwright, producer and public facilitator of grand discussions, who promotes healing dialogue through candid give-and-take. Anyone interested in theatre should see the plays published here performed and engage with them as well-conceived metaphors for the stage, allowing the singular event to stand for the tide of a people responding to a moment of crisis in their history. For anyone interested in the state of Islam in today's world, experiencing these plays should be nothing less than compulsory.

It's exciting to know that Akbar Ahmed's journey as a man of the theatre continues even after the publication of these two fine plays. Next up on the boards is a memoir monologue that Dr Ahmed will perform himself, *From Waziristan to Washington: A Muslim at the Crossroads*, which will receive its official world premiere at Theater J in 2009 as part of its 'Voices From a Changing Middle East' festival. Taken from the annals of Dr Ahmed's own life, the play opens with the advent of 9/11 and the role suddenly thrust upon this leading world authority on Islam who finds himself compelled to explain his culture and history to a hostile Western world. He takes us back to his birthplace and traces the evolution of modern Pakistan, the attempts to integrate with the modern world and the rise of Islamic extremism in the face of Western ignorance. It's a moving multimedia event and the next chapter in this ever-young, ever-fecund, ever-generous author's ever-growing body of work. We are all the richer for Akbar Ahmed's prodigiously illuminating gifts.

Ari Roth
Artistic Director, Theater J
Washington, DC, 2009

NOOR

A Play in Two Acts

Noor means 'light' and is one of the names of 'God' in Arabic. It is popular as a name for both male and female Muslims. In our case, it is the name of an eighteen-year-old college girl. The play takes place in a city in the Muslim world, which could be Baghdad, Cairo, Karachi or Kabul. The Muslims we encounter are typical urban middle-class people. They are overwhelmed by living in a big city with many problems and several layers of conflict – and especially by the chaos of military conflict. The troops kidnapping and killing civilians could be Westerners, but might also be local soldiers trained by Westerners, or shadowy 'insurgents'. The old order is clearly dying out, and a new one is being born. Old ideas are struggling to find new expressions. Society is in a state of disrepair and disruption. The crisis of one family is the crisis of the world.

Dramatis Personae

Abdullah
College lecturer. Thirty-five years old. Wears traditional, nondescript clothes, with a longish white coat over Western-style trousers, a traditional Muslim cap on his head. Has stubble. Married with one child. He is an idealist, a gentle mystic lost in his own world. Eldest brother of Ali, Daoud and Noor.

Daoud
Medical doctor; looks after the poor in his neighbourhood as his 'Islamic' activity. Twenty-six years old. Has a thick, trimmed beard, wears a white skullcap, white tunic and grey loose pyjama-style trousers. Has a perpetual frown on his face and appears tense, though he can smile and show a certain warmth. Passionate and easily moved to emotion.

Father (*Assad Hussein*)
Stocky man in his mid-sixties. Has had a stroke and is not in good health. Unshaven, with a moustache, thick hair and bushy eyebrows. Wears a sweater tucked into his trousers. Worked for the old regime, a nationalist, socialist government, which was ousted and disgraced. Was implicated in a trial and spent some time in jail. We are not sure exactly what he was accused of, but he has never recovered.

Ali
A junior official at a government ministry with dreams of doing well for himself while bringing modern reform to the state. Twenty-seven years old. Wears a suit and tie, which is open and loosened. Has glasses and a moustache. Parts his hair in the middle, and is clean-shaven.

Three soldiers
Tall and muscular, they are dressed in Western-style military fatigues with helmets, goggles, guns, etc. Difficult to tell if they are 'foreign' or local. Even their abuse may be acquired, like their clothes and weapons. They represent arbitrary and excessive state power, using fear and violence indiscriminately: the face of the twenty-first century.

Sheikh Moinuddin
Tall, thin, approximately sixty to sixty-five years old. Has a long white beard and wears loose-fitting white clothes.

Disciple
Has a clipped, whitish beard. Wears loose-fitting, white, worn clothes.

Deputy Minister
Fifty years old. Fat. Wears a tight-fitting Western suit.

Flunky
Wears red livery with yellow sash, plus a turban. Has a waxed moustache.

Auntie Fatima
Father's sister. In her early fifties. Overweight, overdressed and loud.

Fadel
Truck driver. Late twenties. Dishevelled, with shirt hanging out of trousers. Thin. Unshaven.

Noor
Eighteen. Has brown complexion with dark eyes and dark hair. Bright and lively, she is in her first year at a girls' college. Wears blue tunic, loose white pyjamas and a white headscarf.

ACT I

A somewhat rundown lower-middle-class living room. Early morning, before sunrise, during the month of Ramadan. Abdullah enters and switches on the light. He goes to the television set and turns it on. We hear recitation from the Qur'an. Abdullah walks across the stage, looks at the table at the centre of the room and exits into the kitchen. We hear running water and the sounds of crockery and pots and pans being handled.

TV ANNOUNCER (O.S.) God will be kind to those who sacrifice by abstaining from food and water and all that is forbidden, and remembering God during Ramadan. You are the blessed community, the community of Muhammad, peace be upon him. And this is the month when the Qur'an was revealed to the holy Prophet, when God opens the gates of Paradise.

Abdullah re-enters at stage right. He sets the table and appears harassed. Daoud enters through the front door at the left. They speak in hushed tones, both aware that Father might overhear them upstairs.

DAOUD *Assalaam alaikum.*

ABDULLAH *Wa alaikum assalaam.* Come in, come in, Daoud. (*Pause.*) Any news?

DAOUD (*shakes his head*) No, brother.

ABDULLAH Neither one of them?

DAOUD No. Just rumours.

ABDULLAH That's not so good. I was hoping ...

DAOUD Everyone is talking about them in the neighbourhood. Some people saw the whole incident in the bazaar. They may have been taken to the Holiday Inn.

ABDULLAH The Holiday Inn?

DAOUD The Holiday Inn. The final word in hotel comfort.

ABDULLAH What are your people saying?

DAOUD They are saying nothing. They saw nothing, they heard nothing, they know nothing. 'God help you, and goodbye.' The neighbourhood isn't the same anymore; everyone is nervous. Cousins spying on each other, friends reporting on friends, who is there to trust? But God give me patience, I am here to have *sehri* with you and Father before I meet with Imam Khaliq from the mosque.

ABDULLAH (*in and out of kitchen*) I'm making *sehri* now, it just needs to cool off. Where do you keep the sugar? I think we've run out.

DAOUD I am sorry. I'll pick it up from the bazaar sometime today. I'll get an extra two pounds of sugar for you. Do you need anything else?

ABDULLAH Why should I need anything?

DAOUD I know you mystics live on thin air, but brother Abdullah, have you forgotten you have a wife and child?

ABDULLAH Of course, of course. Thank you, Daoud. I will ring home after *sehri* to check that all is well. (*Sighs.*)How soon do you think we will know?

DAOUD Imam Khaliq will find out, *insh'allah*. He knows people everywhere, and is a faithful Muslim. He would not sell his loyalty to any man in uniform or to any Crusader who throws around dollars.

The lights suddenly flicker.

ABDULLAH Not again. Those clumsy contractors are messing with the generators. The power has gone out five times this week.

DAOUD Damned Americans.

ABDULLAH What makes you think they're Americans?

DAOUD Americans are everywhere.

ABDULLAH (*starting for the kitchen*) I heard one that was definitely speaking Spanish.

DAOUD Well damn them, too. They're all Crusaders.

ABDULLAH (O.S.) Daoud, you blame Americans for everything.

DAOUD Because they follow no laws. If a Crusader shoots a child, no one will care ... they'll call the child a 'terrorist', and that will be that. Freedom fighters who are giving their lives for Islam are labelled criminals and insurgents and shot like dogs. One day, *insh'allah*, they will triumph and their deeds will be written in golden letters.

ABDULLAH (*returning from kitchen with food*) Daoud, please go upstairs and see if Father will join us for *sehri*.

Daoud goes upstairs while Abdullah continues to set the table. Daoud returns with Father, walking slowly, sits him in his chair in front of the television and brings a tray of food.

ABDULLAH *Assalaam alaikum*, Father. How are you feeling today?

FATHER I feel so tired and ill all the time. If Noor were here, she would make sure I take the right pills at the right time. When is she coming home?

DAOUD She is with Auntie Aisha, who's not been well. You know Noor, she insisted on staying to look after her.

ABDULLAH We are happy to tend to you in her absence, Father, and she is happy that we may do so. She will return later tonight if Auntie feels better.

FATHER What about the curfew?

DAOUD You are worrying yourself too much, Father. Even in

her illness, our aunt will make sure Noor is safe. She may keep Noor back for another night.

FATHER You know how my little angel reads poetry to me before I go to bed. Just as I used to read to her before bedtime. (*Pauses.*) She never wanted to go to sleep; Mother would sing to her, then she was out like a light. (*Pauses.*) Now, I am the child who must be fussed over, and Noor has no mother to help her to sing me to sleep.

ABDULLAH She will be back shortly. She will read Rumi to you again. My brother is right, Father, all is well.

Smiles, touches Father reassuringly.

Look, I have made your morning meal, and your favourite television programme is on.

FATHER (*tasting food*) What is this?

DAOUD (*almost gently*) Abdullah has worked hard to make it.

FATHER I appreciate your efforts, Abdullah; but see that Noor is back today.

ABDULLAH We will, Father.

Daoud and Abdullah go to the table to eat their meal. Father is engrossed in the television programme.

DAOUD I don't like lying to him, and I don't like having to lie for her.

ABDULLAH It is best we tell him nothing. Have a heart, Daoud; he is an old man, and not well at all. He would not be able to cope with Noor's loss.

DAOUD Well, Noor should have been much more responsible. If she were as modest in manner as in dress, we would not be in this situation.

ABDULLAH Don't blame Noor for her predicament.

DAOUD Our mothers and grandmothers covered their hair in modesty. But they also knew when to keep silent, and when to be seen. They stayed at home and ran the household.

ABDULLAH Modesty is about purity of the soul. Noor is totally innocent. Speaking out about her beliefs is not against Islam, as Islam requires women to play their full role. Do I have to remind you of our mother, God rest her soul, and the great role models we all look to from the Prophet's own family? They were scholars, traders and even commanders of armies in battle.

DAOUD I know, I know. And next you'll remind me that the Prophet said Paradise is at the feet of the mother, and we need to respect women.

ABDULLAH As long as you know what Islam teaches about women, I'm satisfied.

DAOUD If they stay on the true path, there will be no problems, but if they wander off they will find trouble.

ABDULLAH (*changing his tone*) Will you have rice or bread?

DAOUD (*cautiously*) Did you make them yourself ...?

ABDULLAH (*sighs in exasperation*) No. I ordered them from your favourite *kebab* shop.

DAOUD Praise be to God. I'll have both, rice and bread. (*Helps himself to the food.*) There are so many horror stories about what happens to these women.

ABDULLAH Yes, I've heard vaguely.

DAOUD I treated one myself at the hospital the other day. The girl was only fifteen; she was badly bruised, even on the inside. A few of her teeth had been knocked out, and her mouth was bloodied; her nose was broken and bloody as well.

ABDULLAH This is terrible. Terrible.

DAOUD Her father brought her in. He was almost in tears. The bruises would fade, the blood would clot, we could find some false teeth, but could I put her virginity back? Unless a doctor could do that, no one would marry her.

ABDULLAH (*shuddering*) 'Put it back.' That's awful. Is it even possible?

DAOUD It is done. But it is un-Islamic. It broke my heart to tell him how unethical his request was. I demanded to know who had done this to her. He said there was a camp with some ghastly name, 'Paradise Now', something like that, where senior officials pay money for pretty virgins from the Holiday Inn.

ABDULLAH 'Paradise Now.' What a mockery.

DAOUD These girls are auctioned to the highest bidder to become a bride for the night to these villains. Every one of my supervisors at the hospital told me to forget about it. They're all afraid.

ABDULLAH This is worse than I ever imagined.

DAOUD This is reality, brother. I can go on with these stories forever. I remember the haunted looks in the eyes of a young girl who was brought to me by her mother. They had deflowered her, and when she became pregnant they booked her under the adultery laws.

ABDULLAH *Astaghfirallah*. God forgive us.

DAOUD Now the same girl faces the death penalty. Her mother was hysterical because she knew that marriage was out of the question, and now her daughter could lose her life. I pray to God to give me strength when I discover that is where they have taken Noor.

ABDULLAH *If* that is where they have taken Noor. Don't let your imagination run away with you.

DAOUD (*faltering*) Yes ... *if* ... But I'm afraid we will lose our honour.

ABDULLAH You must have faith. I promise you, Noor will be back safely. Safely, and with honour.

DAOUD Your prayers better work fast. If the rumours are true, we are running out of time. These girls only have forty-eight hours to be released or sent off to be dishonoured.

ABDULLAH Why forty-eight hours?

DAOUD They have reduced the sorting-out of female prisoners – the plain ones from the pretty ones – to a fine art. But it takes them two full days to do it. They then decide whom to keep in the Holiday Inn and whom to send to those debauched officials running our so-called Islamic government.

ABDULLAH There is no time to lose. I will see my Sufi *sheikh* straight after prayers. Noor cannot be dishonoured. We will pray for her, and we will pray for all the girls in danger that they may be safe in their homes.

DAOUD Such girls rarely go home.

ABDULLAH What do you mean?

DAOUD Brother, you teachers really live in your own world. Once these girls are dishonoured, their dishonour touches their families, and people prefer the girls not to return.

ABDULLAH I find that difficult to believe.

DAOUD The girls are passed from official to official, and in the end many become prostitutes just to survive.

ABDULLAH Shame. Shame. These poor girls are twice punished: by the beasts who brutalise them, and by their own families, who fail to support them in their hour of need.

DAOUD When it is a matter of honour, people will preserve their own at all cost.

ABDULLAH Noor must come home immediately, and we must do everything to ensure that she feels honoured.

DAOUD She has already dishonoured herself by being taken to a prison run by male sadists. These Crusaders know very well that by dishonouring Noor they dishonour every one of us.

ABDULLAH Daoud, get a grip on yourself.

DAOUD Do you remember how Abu Bakr's daughter killed herself a few months ago, after she was picked up for interrogation? Her sacrifice saved the honour of her family.

ABDULLAH We don't really know the facts about Abu Bakr's daughter.

DAOUD Someone will have to pay for Noor's dishonour. I will see to it.

ABDULLAH I forbid any such discussion, and this line of thinking will not help Noor. I promise you, Noor will return safely if you appeal to God directly from your heart, and there is no better time to ask than before dawn during the month of fasting. It is said God listens to those in pain, and even the angels plead on their behalf.

DAOUD God hasn't been listening to Muslims recently.

ABDULLAH You are mocking faith.

DAOUD I'm not, but God is omnipotent. All-knowing. And He has told us to seize the moment, to translate ideas into actions.

The morning meal is finished. Offstage, the aazan, *or call to prayer, can be heard coming from the neighbourhood mosque.*

AAZAN (O.S.) God is Great ... God is Great ... Come to Prayer ... Come to Prayer ... Come to what is good for you ... Come to what is good for you ...

ABDULLAH *Subhanallah, subhanallah*. God is most exalted. Let us pray, Daoud.

The aazan *drifts to a close. Daoud repeats parts of the* aazan *emphatically while preparing to say his prayers, and takes his position alongside Abdullah, who has removed two prayer mats from a sideboard and is spreading them out. While the two pray side by side, we hear the sound of a car door shutting and an engine revving. Ali enters, wearing his usual business attire comprising dark suit, white shirt and black tie, but looking dishevelled. He has bruises. His eyes are red from lack of sleep, and has evidently not yet had a chance to shave. He takes a few puffs of the cigarette in his mouth, puts it out, then checks his watch and attempts to groom himself a little before fully entering the room. Seeing his brothers at prayer, he takes his shoes off and ties a handkerchief around his head to make a cap; then he joins in the prayers behind them, out of their sight. As prayers finish, Daoud and Abdullah turn and see Ali. They are happy to see him, but are clearly disturbed by his appearance and by the fact that Noor is not with him. They attempt to restrain these emotions in front of Father.*

ALI (*softly and sadly*) *Assalaam alaikum*.

ABDULLAH Ali! Welcome back.

DAOUD Is Noor with you? Where –

ALI Noor ...

ABDULLAH (*cuts him off*) Father, look who is here.

ALI *Assalaam alaikum*, Father.

FATHER Ali! Where have you been? You've missed *sehri*. You look a mess, have you been out all night?

Father closely scrutinises Ali from his recliner. Ali says nothing.

ABDULLAH (*interposing himself between Ali and Father*) You look as though you've been in an accident!

FATHER Are you feeling alright?

ALI (*looking at his brothers*) Yes, an accident. There was an accident.

FATHER I hope you are not injured! Daoud, look after your brother.

ABDULLAH Ali, my brother, are you badly hurt?

DAOUD Those soldier dogs –

ABDULLAH – are such reckless drivers! Every day, someone gets hit by one of their cars. Daoud, do you remember last week, our neighbour Umar –

FATHER Did you see the licence plate? I will call to complain about that driver.

ALI No, it was too dark. It's not a big deal anyhow, I should have seen him coming.

ABDULLAH Father, if you'll excuse us, Daoud and I have some business to discuss with Ali.

Father nods, clearly not satisfied with the reply, and returns to his television. Abdullah and Daoud lead Ali to the dining table. Daoud attempts to inspect Ali's wounds discreetly.

ALI Is there any news?

ABDULLAH News? I thought you had the news ... Where is she? And what happened to you? Are you alright?

ALI I'm fine. So you haven't told Father yet?

ABDULLAH No, nothing.

ALI Is it really necessary to lie to him? He will start to get suspicious.

DAOUD No one has ever suffered a stroke from suspicion; but the truth could kill him.

ABDULLAH How did you manage to escape, Ali? Tell us, could the truth be worse than anything we suspect?

DAOUD Is it true what the neighbours have said, that you were taken from the bazaar?

ALI Yes.

ABDULLAH Are you fasting, should I get you something to eat?

ALI Thank you, brother. No, I'm not fasting. I haven't been eating properly.

ABDULLAH Okay, I'll get you some food. I'm so happy you're back safely.

Abdullah exits to kitchen.

DAOUD How could you have allowed your own sister to stand around in the bazaar? I'm not blaming you, Ali, but you know that violence can happen anytime there.

ALI (*defensively*) She insisted she would buy grapes for Father.

DAOUD Grapes ...

ABDULLAH (*enters with a plate of food, hearing the conversation*) Well, it is his favourite fruit. He's always loved fresh grapes to open the fast.

DAOUD Women. Noor is just like Mother. She always wants to spoil Father.

ABDULLAH She was just being kind. Indulging him. He's not been well.

DAOUD (*impatiently*) And damaging him. Grapes become

sugar in his blood, and his diabetes is out of control. He refuses to take the *yunani* medicine that I want him to take. And the side effects of these Western medicines he insists on taking can be deadly.

ABDULLAH It is the special month of Ramadan. At least stop being a doctor during these days.

DAOUD Father can't fast now. To think, the family honour was exposed for some grapes! The fruit that produces wine, the forbidden drink in Islam. And there's a good reason why God forbade –

ABDULLAH (*smiling*) Please, Daoud.

ALI (*flaring up*) They were just grapes!

DAOUD But what about Noor? Did they hurt her?

ALI They yelled at her; Noor answered back, and they became very angry.

ABDULLAH They probably felt challenged.

DAOUD Who yelled at her? Who were they? They must have been Americans.

ABDULLAH How can you be sure?

DAOUD Who else is so barbaric?

ALI They were dressed in military fatigues and had modern-looking guns and wore dark glasses like American soldiers. They swore a lot. But I'm sure they were our people.

ABDULLAH Yes, our own soldiers dress the same way.

DAOUD Did they hurt her?

ALI They shoved her ... she said something ... and I saw one of them slap her. I tried to rush to her, but they kept me back. I've never felt such a fire in my blood.

DAOUD They abused Noor? They actually hit a woman? These

barbarians have no shame; I'll make them pay for this!

ABDULLAH (*gesturing towards Father*) Quiet, brother. Calm yourself.

DAOUD (*calming down*) Did she cry? She never shows fear.

ALI She was shaking with rage, and trying to control her tears. She has so much pride.

DAOUD She is a brave daughter of Islam.

ALI She provoked the soldiers, called them 'bullies' and 'cowards' and 'traitors to our country'. She even accused them of not being real men because they fight defenceless women. I kept telling her to be quiet ... they pulled us apart and gagged and blindfolded us. We were then pushed into separate jeeps and driven off.

ABDULLAH They gagged you?

ALI Yes.

ABDULLAH Didn't you tell them you're a lawyer? A trained lawyer?

ALI I did.

ABDULLAH And did that make a difference?

ALI (*bitterly*) Actually, that's when they gagged me ...

DAOUD I'm so sorry to hear this, my brother. What about the onlookers? Didn't anyone try to prevent this?

ALI No. It all happened so fast ... everyone seemed to be shocked, dazed. There had been an explosion only a few hours before, and people had died. Everyone was nervous, including the authorities.

ABDULLAH When emotions are high, people become unreasonable. These soldiers are little more than boys.

DAOUD That's no excuse for this barbaric behaviour.

ALI Either we belong to a civilised society or we live in a jungle.

DAOUD These Americans have reduced Muslim societies to a jungle. But even the jungle has certain laws. Here we don't have any. Only Islam can prevent our societies from completely collapsing. Brother, were you –?

ALI No. They threatened to. But no. No.

ABDULLAH Praise be to God. I am a sinner. But Noor is pure. God will listen to me. I prayed and will seek the prayers of my *sheikh*.

DAOUD The prayers of the *sheikh* will achieve nothing. God says you must take action with your own hands. Pray to Him, but tie your camel, those are the words of the Prophet. *Insh'allah*, the time of justice is near.

ABDULLAH Please, brother ... there is too much violence, too much blood already.

DAOUD (*to Ali*) You still haven't told us how you escaped, brother.

ALI Escape? There was no escape. They let me go when they realised they had nothing on me. I pleaded with them to tell me about Noor, but they were heartless. They wouldn't even let me make a single call.

DAOUD And you have no idea where Noor is?

ALI (*sighing*) No. After I have eaten and washed, I will go to the Ministry of Justice. I know the secretary to the Deputy Minister, I shouldn't need an appointment.

DAOUD Bureaucrats ... they're useless.

ABDULLAH This is not encouraging. I had hoped you could tell us something we did not already know.

DAOUD Did you not demand the guards to tell you where she was?

ALI Of course I did. But the guards don't listen to prisoners. I am sure I will find out where she is from the minister's office.

DAOUD What makes you think that this minister will be any different, Ali?

ALI We must appeal to him. He can help if he wants to. What options do we have?

DAOUD We can do more ... we must not accept Noor's fate.

ABDULLAH No one is saying we have to accept her fate. But we must never do what is wrong in order to make something right.

DAOUD Look around you, Abdullah. There is chaos everywhere, anarchy. Our own Noor has been dishonoured, but *no* Noor is safe anywhere.

ABDULLAH Yes, brother, it is true that Muslims are suffering. *Insh'allah*, our Noor will be back unharmed and safe. Still, we must pray for every Noor in every home, wherever she is.

DAOUD Yes, yes, but I cannot ignore what is happening to my people any more. We Muslims are being killed and tortured and humiliated across the world. We have been robbed of our honour and dignity. Entire generations are growing up traumatised and angry at the injustices, and yet Muslims are being called 'terrorists' and 'extremists'. And everywhere America is leading the attack on Islam. Islam is under siege. It is time for every Muslim to stand up and say, 'No more. We will not take this any more. We will be heard.'

ABDULLAH Revenge and hatred will not repair our broken hearts. There has been too much rupture. Too many tragedies. Too many tears have been shed. We must feel for the pain of others. I was deeply saddened to hear about the attack on the old Christian church in our city last month. I even heard a rumour that some Christian girls had been molested.

DAOUD Christians molested? This is just propaganda put out by the Crusaders to justify their acts. Brother, you are far too concerned with the suffering of others.

ABDULLAH You forget the special regard our holy Prophet had for Christians. That is why he sent those persecuted Muslims from Mecca to the Christian kingdom in Africa. These Christians living amongst us are a peaceful minority and deserve our full sympathy.

ALI (*angry*) Daoud, I would have thought that Noor's disappearance would make you more sympathetic to the things she believes in. I can take pride in saying that she shares my ideas. Noor's ideas about women's rights are inspired by my talks to her about human rights.

DAOUD She doesn't share your ideas. She is a good and pious Muslim. I have been talking to her, and she will become a doctor, *insh'allah*, and help me with my work. She is dedicated to the cause of Islam.

ABDULLAH Please, brothers, it's the special time of the fast. Let us not argue. I want all of us to come together as a family to think of the blessings of God. To find strength in our prayers.

The brothers sit quietly.

ALI Abdullah, you remind me so much of Mother right now. I thank God she has been spared the agony of this world. He has been most merciful.

DAOUD There may be mercy for the dead; there is none left for the living.

ALI Sometimes I am not inclined to believe you, Daoud.

But no, you are right. Our mother has been spared much sorrow. At times, I envy her.

DAOUD She was a saint.

ABDULLAH And you, Daoud, were her constant tormentor.

DAOUD I was not. I loved her just as much as you did.

ABDULLAH That may be true, but you forget all the times our neighbours called to complain to her about you. Auntie Fatima would rush over in a huff to tell Mother how you had taunted her poor son.

ALI (*in a mock Auntie Fatima voice*) The little rat has torn Rahman's shirt and given him a black eye! Is this how he treats his future brother-in-law? Just you wait until Rahman has grown, that is the day the tables will turn!

The brothers laugh.

ABDULLAH She always complained about how delicate her baby was.

DAOUD Fifteen years later, and he is as delicate as he was when he was a boy ... but for Noor's sake, I've left him alone.

ALI Just imagine, by this time next year, Noor and Rahman will be happily married.

ABDULLAH If only Mother were alive to see that day.

Suddenly there is loud knocking and much noise. Three fully armed soldiers burst into the house.

FIRST SOLDIER Everybody, on the floor face down, hands on your head!

FATHER Officers, I am a retired senior government official, how may I –

FIRST SOLDIER On the floor, old man! And keep your fucking mouth shut!

The soldiers push the family to the floor with their hands behind their backs.

SECOND SOLDIER (*as though reading a well-rehearsed, scripted monologue*) We have received information that persons unknown in this area have been working with the insurgents. If you know someone who is involved in terrorist-related activity, you are advised under the law to give us their names and whereabouts. We will need to search your house for illegal weapons.

FATHER We are *not* insurgents, we are law-abiding citizens.

FIRST SOLDIER Shut the fuck up! (*Gesturing to the second soldier.*) You, search upstairs!

The second soldier heads upstairs.

DAOUD What is going on? What do you want?

ABDULLAH We are peaceful people, we've done nothing wrong. Please tell us how we can assist.

THIRD SOLDIER We're not going to harm you. We're looking for information on terrorists. There have been reports that girls in this neighbourhood are aiding the insurgency.

DAOUD This is our family home, and we are respectable people. You must leave now, you'll find nothing here.

FIRST SOLDIER What do we have here? A cheeky monkey. Keep your mouth shut, I'm warning you. Put your head down!

FATHER This is unacceptable! Ali, tell them what our rights are!

Ali does not speak.

Ali, tell them!

FIRST SOLDIER Rights? You have no rights, this is a question of national security. How do we know you're not a motherfucking terrorist?

FATHER (*beginning to stand*) Don't abuse me. How can you speak to me in this manner?

FIRST SOLDIER (*kicks Father back down to the floor*) Hey. Down on the floor.

DAOUD Don't you dare touch my father. Have you no mercy? He is very ill.

THIRD SOLDIER So you're a doctor, are you? Just follow instructions, so we can do our job and leave. We're keeping the peace around here.

FATHER 'Keeping the peace.' You have violated my home, tracked mud onto my carpet –

FIRST SOLDIER (*pushing his boot into Father's face*) You're so concerned about mud? Lick it off my boots, then!

DAOUD Father! (*Daoud struggles to rise. The first soldier strikes his head with the butt of his rifle.*)

SECOND SOLDIER (*returning with papers*) Hey guys, look what I found hidden under some shirts!

Reads from one of the papers.

'Muslim women demand rights.' 'We see nothing but injustice and corruption around us.'

THIRD SOLDIER What's that?

SECOND SOLDIER It's from a college essay.

FIRST SOLDIER We have a real firecracker here. Terrorist bitch.

SECOND SOLDIER She wants her 'rights'.

FIRST SOLDIER (*gesturing crudely*) Yeah, come to Papa, baby, I'll give you your rights!

SECOND SOLDIER We've got what we wanted. Come on, we've got at least ten more houses in this neighbourhood.

The first soldier, with a sweep of his rifle, knocks everything off the mantelpiece behind the table, family photographs included – along with them is a portrait of the brothers' mother. The first soldier notices the photograph, and picks it up.

FIRST SOLDIER Ugh, take a look at this ugly bitch. She's got a bigger moustache than our captain.

The first soldier throws the picture to the floor. All three soldiers then exit just as suddenly as they came in. Abdullah rushes to help Father off the floor. Daoud rushes to Father as well, in order to make sure that he is not hurt. Ali remains on the floor, traumatised. Father insists he's alright, but holds his side in pain.

FATHER What were they doing in my house? Who are these girls they were looking for?

ABDULLAH God knows what they wanted.

FATHER Are they looking for Noor? Is that why she is with Auntie Aisha? She's hiding from them? God help us if they find her. We must call Auntie Aisha right this minute. I must speak to her, warn her.

ABDULLAH Father, please, don't get excited.

FATHER Abdullah, I order you, go upstairs and get my diary, Aisha's phone number should be there. Daoud, bring me the phone.

ABDULLAH Father, you need to rest. I will talk to Auntie Aisha about Noor.

FATHER Don't coddle me, get me a phone.

ABDULLAH Later, Father, later. After you've rested.

DAOUD We will call Auntie Aisha, once we're sure you're alright.

FATHER Later? Later? What if they find her?! Oh God, what if they already have her ...? They took things from her room to use as evidence. Would they do that? Would they come here to get evidence if they already had her?

DAOUD Remember your blood pressure.

ABDULLAH (*to Daoud*) Check Father, Daoud.

FATHER To hell with my blood pressure, I want to know where my daughter is! Aren't you boys in the least bit concerned? Soldiers come tramping through here, they take your sister's things, and Ali, who takes such pride in his appearance, is sitting here looking like ...

Pauses, comes to a realisation.

There was no accident, was there?

ALI (*meekly*) I was walking along the road, a car came up behind me, they didn't have their headlights on ...

FATHER There was no accident.

ALI I fell onto the road, the driver never even saw me —

FATHER There was *no accident*, Ali! All lies! (*Picks up the photo that had been thrown to the floor.*) I'm still the head of this household! Don't hide things from me! Do you think I'm senile?

ABDULLAH Father, none of us ever said that.

FATHER (*thrusting the photo into Ali's face*) There! Swear on your mother's honour that everything you have said is true!

Ali holds the photo, looking at it as though he is lost.

FATHER Speak.

ABDULLAH Father, I can vouch for what Ali said.

FATHER Let him speak for himself.

DAOUD Ali, tell Father what happened. You might as well. Father, we were just protecting you ...

ALI Soldiers abducted Noor and me at the bazaar. I was bringing her back from the college when she insisted we buy grapes for you. They came out of nowhere ... They blindfolded me, they – I couldn't see where they took her. They took me to the central jail. No one talks. They kept us sealed off, cut off from one another. If you talk, you're beaten. Finally, I persuaded them that I was a law-abiding citizen and they decided to release me. I washed and changed out of those stinking prison clothes and came home to plan to get Noor out.

Puts down the photo.

That is all I know. I promise you, Father, in the name of my mother. This is simply an isolated miscarriage of justice, that is all.

FATHER That is all? When a man with a gun puts his dirty boot on your father's face, when these pigs insult your mother, when your own sister has been abducted, is maybe being dishonoured as we speak, you say 'that is all'? My sons are useless!

Father looks angrily at his sons, and shuffles out of the room as if an immense weight was upon him. He is on the verge of tears.

ABDULLAH We did what we thought was right. No one can fault us for that.

ALI They teach you to lie in law school, but they never taught me how to swear on my mother's honour.

DAOUD Where were your elegant legal speeches when they told Father to lick the mud off their boots?

Turns to Abdullah.

And you! What did your saints say to drive them off?

ABDULLAH The saints give us inspiration and hope, not grenades and explosives, Daoud.

DAOUD The two of you, lying there like lambs while they violate our home!

ALI The less one says the better. Would you have challenged them any further? Given them a reason to stick around and maybe take us all to prison?

DAOUD You're frightened of prison? People like you who talk about the law are not prepared to sacrifice one drop of blood to uphold it. It is the ordinary Muslim who sacrifices his life and his property for our freedom and honour. It is he who is preventing a proud and independent people from being turned into a slave nation. With his blood, my brother, not fine legal phrases.

ABDULLAH Please be quiet, both of you, and help me clean this place up.

Daoud's pager begins to vibrate.

DAOUD Let me take this call.

Daoud goes off to the kitchen.

ABDULLAH That is just so typical of him.

Ali stays where he is.

ALI I didn't even know who they were. They could have been anybody. They could have been us.

ABDULLAH (*stops cleaning, crosses to Ali*) God have mercy on us. We live in an age without a soul.

ALI These people have no idea of mercy or justice.

ABDULLAH No one is immune to God's justice. God's name *is* Justice.

Pauses.

Ali, you are not yourself.

ALI (*bursts out*) Of course I am not! I have been trained to uphold the ideals of justice, the only thing that separates us from the animals! I am supposed to fight with my pen and my words, fight for what God has decreed and society has written into law. What good are we if we can't implement the law on earth? What good am I? We have no rights. We are vulnerable anytime and anywhere. Anyone can walk into our homes and humiliate us. Even our women are not safe.

ABDULLAH Who are these people, Ali? Are they outsiders, or our own people?

ALI Sometimes it's hard to tell. The men who interrogated me were our own, I could tell from their dialect. But there was also a foreigner. He had dark glasses, a blue blazer and a crew cut. He didn't speak much, but the guards were terrified of him ... Do you know what they could be doing to Noor right now as we speak?

ABDULLAH I thank God that you have come back to us safely. God is compassionate and merciful. He will look after Noor.

ALI (*breaks down and begins to cry*) I fear for her. There was no compassion or mercy in what I saw.

ABDULLAH (*softly*) Tell me what you saw.

ALI If any harm came to Noor I don't know what I would do with myself. I felt so helpless, so powerless.

ABDULLAH You are not to blame. Tell me everything, it will help you lighten your burden. Talk to me Ali, and get it off your chest.

ALI I can't.

ABDULLAH Trust me, the pain you feel will be removed. Go back to your prison cell and tell me what you saw.

After a pause, Ali slowly sinks to the floor. In quiet, hard tones he begins to speak. Abdullah sits down by him and puts his arm around him.

ALI I was in a cold dank, dark, basement room. They made me take off my clothes. They laughed at my nakedness. Women took pictures of me. The guards beat me and the blood crawled down my body and froze on me like a second skin.

ABDULLAH God have mercy on us. Go on Ali, go on. I am here with you.

ALI (*sobbing*) They called me a terrorist, a dog, a pig. I urinated and defecated, chained like a beast. I was losing my mind. I was terrified that I would be forgotten and left in that hell-hole forever. They called me women's names. They praised my 'soft skin'. (*Mimicking the soldiers.*) 'Tighten the collar around his neck and bring me my rod. Let's make the pretty little pig squeal.' (*In his normal voice, tearfully.*) I didn't even know I could scream like that, that such pain exists ...

ABDULLAH Any man would scream while being beaten.

ALI They didn't *beat* me with it, Abdullah.

Pauses.

They even use those monstrous dogs ... Alsatians. Filthy, hairy beasts. They use them on women too; I could hear it ... can you imagine ... dogs.

Ali breaks down sobbing. Abdullah just holds him like a child for a few moments.

ABDULLAH (*softly*) May God embrace you in his compassion. How do you feel now?

ALI I feel better. Thank you, brother, for sharing my pain.

ABDULLAH (*quietly*) Noor is in great danger.

Abdullah gathers himself together, preparing to go out.

ALI Where are you going?

ABDULLAH Where else can I go? To see Sheikh Moinuddin in person. The *sheikh* must use his spiritual powers to get Noor back. What I've heard has confirmed the sickness that I've feared in the souls of men. I've already been leaving messages for him, but I cannot wait any longer.

ALI What will you tell him?

ABDULLAH I will tell him the truth. These men may have penetrated my family. I will tell him that my sister has been kidnapped, my father's home ransacked, soldiers have humiliated my father and my brother has been ...

Ali gives Abdullah a telling look.

ABDULLAH I must remain calm. I will not let my anger violate *me* as well. And you? What time will you leave for the Ministry of Justice?

ALI The Deputy Minister won't arrive until after the Friday prayers.

Abdullah embraces Ali as he would a child. Abdullah exits. Ali sits quietly for a while and composes himself. Daoud enters, looking around the room cautiously.

DAOUD Where is our elder brother?

ALI (*takes time to reply*) He has gone to see how he can bring Noor back.

DAOUD Oh, the Sufi is off to slay the dragon with the sword

of love in one hand and the shield of compassion in the other.

ALI He thinks his Sufi master can help.

DAOUD Yes, I can picture his *sheikh* twirling and whirling in a trance outside the prison camp. I am sure it will melt the hearts of the guards. We need *warriors*, not mystics. We need Saladin, not Rumi.

ALI We need both! Besides, Sufis are harmless ... At least Abdullah is doing something to get Noor back. All you've done is ridicule your brothers and contest every viable option without giving us an alternative. What do you suggest, Daoud? Tell me.

DAOUD (*angrily*) I've been working *non-stop* to get the two of you back! I haven't slept since we heard the news.

ALI And what exactly did you do all that time, Daoud?

DAOUD Don't take that accusatory tone with me.

ALI I didn't. Just because you couldn't fight the soldiers doesn't mean you have to fight me.

DAOUD You're hardly in a position to talk ... you had no honour in the face of these savages who invaded our home. I suppose your way is best? Blindly believing in a system that doesn't even exist?

ALI We are struggling to create a modern society with law and order, justice and education for everyone. This is the true *jihad*, my *jihad*.

DAOUD The Prophet's *jihad* means fighting for women and children if they are being attacked. Just look at yesterday's paper: wedding party massacred in Kandahar, girls' school in Karbala blown up, genocide in Chechnya ... did you see the photo of the mother holding her dead child in Gaza? Look for yourself!

Holds up a newspaper for Ali.

The boy was on his way to school when an airstrike took his life. Wherever you look, the *ummah* is bleeding. We must defend the *ummah*. *That* is my *jihad*, the true *jihad*.

ALI We've argued about this a hundred times, and you know that for the Prophet the greatest *jihad* is to improve oneself spiritually. Your friends, the ignorant *mullahs*, have reduced this noble concept to a joke so that they can go to Paradise and claim their seventy-two virgins. Or is it eighty-two these days? Where do they even get these figures? Definitely not the Qur'an.

DAOUD The Prophet himself promised that the martyr will inherit Paradise and be served by *houris*.

ALI You forget that his most important saying on martyrdom refers to scholarship: 'The ink of the scholar is more sacred than the blood of the martyr.'

DAOUD This talk of learning and knowledge is just to divert Muslims from their real problems. This soft version of Islam is promoted by those in the West who claim to have the interests of Muslims at heart.

ALI There are many sincere and good people in the West interested in our problems.

DAOUD You're too fascinated by corrupt American culture ever since your trip to the land of the Great Satan.

ALI What is your problem with Americans?

DAOUD What is your infatuation with them? I don't understand. Americans hate Islam. Haven't you heard of Guantánamo? Forget Abu Ghraib. Americans call the holy Prophet a terrorist and paedophile.

ALI That is disgraceful, I accept; but such abuse is rare. Americans are good people who are given bad information. They're frightened, just like us. But freedom and inclusion are in their history. Take the examples of Washington and Jefferson ...

DAOUD (*in a flash of anger*) Washington, Jefferson? Have you forgotten your own heroes? What about Rasul Allah, our beloved Prophet? What about Abu Bakr and Umar and Ali? They were truer to your ideals of justice and compassion than these Crusaders. Umar went out every night, in disguise, to see if people were in pain or hungry. And the Prophet, in his humility, stitched his own clothes. Washington and Jefferson indeed. These Americans, they have no past like us.

ALI But they have a future.

DAOUD The West can give us nothing. Its culture is decadent. Look at how shamelessly Western women behave.

ALI You have a filthy mind; every woman for you is a sex object.

DAOUD Every Western woman *is* a sex object. You know what it's like over there ...

Pauses.

There are even bars where naked women sit on men's laps to pleasure them. Worse are the bars where men do the same for other men. There are shows with girls exposing their private parts just for the fun of it. Shameless behaviour. The Internet is full of it.

ALI What are you doing looking at pornography on the Internet?! You need the modern world; you need the Internet to send your electrocardiograms to other hospitals, the sanitary and sterile instruments.

DAOUD That is different. That is not the modern world, it is in accordance with Islam.

ALI You act like anything coming from the West is an attack on you. Being a part of the modern world does not have to mean giving up who we are.

DAOUD You are *always* trying to give up who you are. I am working with my heart and soul in our community. I share their pain. I tend to their sick and dying and help as much as I possibly can. What are you prepared to give?

ALI I will not allow you to belittle me and my work, Daoud. I am trying against all odds to improve a system that is corrupt and decaying. I am following in Father's footsteps, trying to complete his unfulfilled dreams.

DAOUD Oh, yeah? And how far has that got you? As far as the Holiday Inn.

ALI It is you who is out of touch ... all you know how to do is curse 'Crusaders' and talk about your 'honour'. You're not going to get Noor out by talking ... what are you going to do, Daoud? What are you going to do?

DAOUD (*angrily*) I will avenge Noor. My network can reach places you didn't even know existed.

ALI Oh, I'm shaking with excitement to hear about your network.

DAOUD Suppose I tell you that I know that the American consul goes shopping every Sunday morning? She goes with her painted face and tight clothes to the refugee market. They charge her outrageous prices, she tosses her money around freely while our sister is ... Her driver attends my mosque, and we know exactly when and where she will be.

ALI Have you gone completely mad? What sort of plan is this? It's tribal and barbaric, and I can assure you all of America will be outraged; our own government will descend upon us like a ton of bricks ...

DAOUD I'm not saying this is what *I'm* going to be doing, it's just one of the things that's been discussed. God will decide what is best, *insh'allah*.

ALI Okay, Daoud ... good, I'm glad, because taking any such hostage would be completely idiotic. I am fed up with all those illiterate *mullahs*, those self-appointed champions of Islam, creating more problems for all Muslims. All this nonsensical talk of creating 'terror' in the hearts of the 'Crusaders'.

DAOUD They are weak and cowardly. We don't have the tanks and planes, but we can strike terror through individual acts. They are so concerned about one American death that every newspaper will talk about nothing but that. Just look at what happened after that American Jew was killed in Karachi. *Every* American knew our fury.

ALI That American, too, had a mother and a father. Your hatred has distorted you. You're still following the teachings of that narrow-minded *mullah*. I knew by the time I was ten he was a bigot, and so are you. You blame the Jews for everything.

DAOUD The Qur'an tells us to fight them.

ALI Yes, and to fight Christians or Muslims or people from Mars, anyone who is attacking your families. But you know very well that the next line says: 'Make peace if they want peace, because God prefers peace.'

DAOUD You don't understand Islam. You are corrupted by the West.

ALI You were jealous of me from childhood.

DAOUD Jealous of you? You're pathetic. You so-called lawyer who stood around and let his sister be kidnapped.

ALI And you're a so-called doctor who stood around and let his mother die.

DAOUD How dare you ...

ALI You and your stupid *yunani* medicine ...

DAOUD (*enraged*) You ...!

Daoud lunges towards his brother, but is interrupted as Father enters.

FATHER Stop it, you two. Ali, get me a glass of water and put on some tea.

The lights flicker.

ALI Yes, Father.

Ali exits. Father settles himself into the recliner. Daoud's cell phone rings. He walks to the corner, so Father can't hear, and answers.

DAOUD Hello? (*Listens in silence for a few moments.*) Yes ... yes ... thank you. Thank you so much. (*Disconnects.*)

FATHER Noor?

DAOUD Yes.

FATHER Your contacts?

DAOUD Yes.

FATHER Speak up, son. What have you heard? Is she safe?

DAOUD She's still at the Holiday Inn.

FATHER Is she still in danger?

DAOUD I don't know, Father.

FATHER Will she be shifted?

DAOUD The guard said she is 'too pretty' for the Holiday Inn.

FATHER What does that mean? What can we do?

DAOUD Trust me, Father, I promise I'll fix everything. Everything will be like it was.

FATHER Like it was, my son.

DAOUD No matter the cost.

ACT II

SCENE ONE

At stage left is a divan, raised six inches and about three feet by six feet wide, with red bolsters about three feet long and two small, round pillows on which Sheikh Moinuddin reclines, looking distant. He wears a loose-fitting white shirt, loose white pyjamas and no cap, and has his feet on the divan. A disciple to his right fusses about, straightening Sheikh Moinuddin's slippers. At stage right is a different location: a large bare desk with four telephones on it lined up in a row, and lots of pens also in a row. The Deputy Minister sits behind the desk. He is fat, pompous- looking, with a little moustache but otherwise clean-shaven, wearing a dark suit. His hair is combed back neatly, though he is beginning to go bald. He stares straight ahead.

DISCIPLE — Your disciple Abdullah is here to see you, Sheikh Moinuddin.

Sheikh Moinuddin nods to acknowledge his presence. The disciple places Sheikh Moinuddin's slippers in front of him so the Sheikh may step into them, and then grabs a green velvet robe hanging on the wall and helps Sheikh Moinuddin into it, careful to never turn his back to the master. Finally Sheikh Moinuddin puts on his white cap and motions for the disciple to lead Abdullah in. At stage right, the telephone rings.

DEPUTY MINISTER — (*answering phone*) Yes?

As the Deputy Minister answers the phone, Abdullah enters at stage left, kisses Sheikh Moinuddin's right hand and sits quietly at his feet.

DEPUTY MINISTER — Have you confirmed the tickets yet? I hope you didn't book us on the same airline as before. The stewardess refused to give me the front seat; she said it was for some other VIP. (*Pauses, listening to reply.*).Who could be more important than the Deputy Minister of Justice?!

SHEIKH MOINUDDIN (*to Abdullah*) I have been thinking about your problem.

DEPUTY MINISTER From now on I will only fly with airlines that show the proper respect to our nationals.

The Deputy Minister hangs up and resumes staring out into space, picking his ears.

ABDULLAH You already know?

SHEIKH MOINUDDIN You didn't have to tell me; it is my job to know these things.

ABDULLAH I never doubted your wisdom.

SHEIKH MOINUDDIN Your brother Daoud is not the only one with a far-reaching network.

ABDULLAH A man can only bear so much, my Sheikh. I am here to seek your prayers, as God has not listened to me.

SHEIKH MOINUDDIN I have already prayed for you. Noor will be safe. She will be with you soon, *insh'allah.*

The flunky enters at stage right, places a file on the Deputy Minister's desk and then exits, careful not to show his back. The Deputy Minister looks at it and then pushes it aside, quite uninterested.

ABDULLAH I have lost my mother. My father is very ill. And now, Noor. I need your blessings and your prayers; I feel as though I am standing in deep and dangerous quicksand, slowly sinking in.

SHEIKH MOINUDDIN 'Seek help in patience and prayer.' The Qur'an teaches us how to face every adversity. *Insh'allah*, everything will be all right in the end. God is merciful.

DISCIPLE Even the mightiest in this land come to pay homage to our Sheikh at the *dhikr* session on Thursday night. Last night the Sheikh spoke to his disciple, the Deputy Superintendent of Prisons. Your work, brother Abdullah, will soon be done, *insh'allah.*

The flunky enters at stage right, hands the Deputy Minister a piece of paper, then exits. The Deputy Minister glances at it and grimaces. The flunky enters again.

FLUNKY Shall I show him in, sir?

The Deputy Minister nods. The flunky exits, returns with Ali in tow and exits again.

DEPUTY MINISTER Please, sit. I don't have much time. I am preparing to leave with a delegation to the US, and while I am there I'm going to have a medical checkup. My health isn't what it used to be. So much work; unending pressure.

ALI I am sorry to hear that.

DEPUTY MINISTER What is the nature of your problem?

ALI My name is Ali Hussein. I work for the Ministry of Justice in the legal research department, and I have come to you for assistance. I've brought a petition for my sister's release. For some reason, she and I were both seized in the bazaar and thrown into prison; they let me go, but I still have not been able to locate her. I understand that you are busy, but –

DEPUTY MINISTER Oh yes, I am extremely busy Mr ... Mr ... and I have to say this is nothing new to me. Let me see your application.

SHEIKH MOINUDDIN (*to Abdullah*) We have failed to develop the *ruh*, the soul, and so we find ourselves reaching out in the darkness, hoping to find something to hold onto.

DEPUTY MINISTER (*to Ali*) I get at least a hundred of these every day. My sister. My husband. My cousin, and even my sister's husband's cousin! It just goes on and on. So what can I say? I will do my best, but I am not a miracle worker.

SHEIKH MOINUDDIN (*to Abdullah*) Our masters have told us how God created Adam and then, with the birth of Noor-i-

Muhammadi, He introduced the notion of sharing His divine mercy and compassion with humanity itself. God is light, Abdullah; Noor and our souls reflect His light. Our own Noor is therefore something greater than her physical body. Noor can never be violated because of the purity of her soul.

DEPUTY MINISTER (*to Ali*) That is my burden in life, I suppose: to have so many depend on me, but to be understood by so few. This is a thankless job, Ali. I know my good friends the Americans will give me a tough time with questions of democracy, but they do not understand our society. Democracy needs time, and our people are not used to it.

ALI Sir, my sister ... My father was also in government service. Sir, his health is not good. He has had a stroke and ever since my sister's disappearance, I fear for him.

DEPUTY MINISTER I see. The problem is urgent.(*Pauses.*) You know, there are other ways of getting her out.

ALI I beg your pardon, sir, I am not sure – what other ways are there? I'll do anything to get my sister out.

DEPUTY MINISTER (*abruptly*) Why don't you see my assistant, Razzaq, and all will be clear.

The Deputy Minister rings a bell, and the flunky reappears.

ALI Sir, I was hoping you yourself would –

FLUNKY Sir?

DEPUTY MINISTER Take my visitor to Razzaq, and tell him I sent him.

ALI But, sir ...

DEPUTY MINISTER (*standing up and extending his hand*) Good luck, young man. I have a meeting with the Minister in a few minutes.

A telephone rings; the Deputy Minister answers and begins to talk.

ABDULLAH (*to Sheikh Moinuddin*) You have revived my spirit, o Sheikh. I had begun to feel that the light in my life was flickering, and the darkness at the edges was taunting me.

SHEIKH MOINUDDIN (*handing prayer beads to Abdullah*) Repeat the names of God and that will protect you. God is Compassionate, Merciful, God is Noor, He is Light. This will bring solace to us, and strengthen our belief.

Abdullah, Sheikh Moinuddin and the disciple begin to chant and hum in unison, swaying gently.

Ya Allah hu
Ya Allah hu
God is Compassionate
God is Merciful
Ya Rahmano
Ya Rahimo
Ya Allah hu
Ya Allah hu.

From stage right, Ali *crosses upstage. As the lights dim on the Deputy Minister, Ali lights up a cigarette, lost in thought and frustrated with the result of his meeting.*

SCENE TWO

The next day, mid-morning, in the same living room as in Act I. The three brothers are talking around the table. They are fasting, having had their morning meal a few hours earlier. Things are slow. They await news.

ABDULLAH Have faith in the prayers of the Sufi saint. He has never disappointed anyone in pain or trouble.

ALI Your Sufi saint doesn't have twenty thousand dollars, does he?

ABDULLAH No, but he has something more effective, the power of prayer. The saint's blessings bring miracles.

DAOUD God is the miracle worker, not your Sufi 'saint'.

ALI I knew the country was corrupt, but I had no idea how deep the rot has become. Imagine the Minister of Justice hinting openly for money.

DAOUD Open your eyes, Ali, nothing happens around here unless you bribe someone.

ALI But to me, a government –

DAOUD It doesn't matter ... God is great.

Auntie Fatima enters. The brothers rise from their seats.

AUNTIE FATIMA No, no, don't get up, boys. I'm not going to stay long.

DAOUD *Assalaam alaikum.*

ABDULLAH Auntie, are you fasting? Can I get you some tea?

AUNTIE FATIMA I would love a cup of tea, but you know, my son, we Muslims must bear the burden of the fast even when we are ill.

ABDULLAH Such a pleasure to see you, Auntie. Shall I get Father?

AUNTIE FATIMA No, my son, I'd like to speak to you first.

ALI Is something the matter, Auntie?

AUNTIE FATIMA I must be frank with you, my children, I've always treated you like my own sons. Noor has been like my daughter, and from her birth I've always wanted her to marry my son Rahman.

DAOUD And she will, *insh'allah.* We are all looking forward to the wedding.

AUNTIE FATIMA I must be blunt. I don't mean to be cruel. I've been hearing nasty rumours. Everyone is talking about what happened in the bazaar. My neighbours have been taunting me. They say Noor's honour has been violated.

ALI Auntie, how could you say this? You are like her mother!

AUNTIE FATIMA I'm sorry, my children, but these rumours have made Rahman into a laughing-stock. His friends are ridiculing him. They're saying he will get 'soiled goods'.

DAOUD How dare these shameless men speak in this manner! Don't they have sisters of their own?!

AUNTIE FATIMA My poor boy Rahman has been distraught. He does love Noor so, but he is concerned about his job. He is doing so well in accounting, and he works for this top American firm. He needs to be careful about his reputation. This situation is casting a shadow over him.

ABDULLAH What exactly are you getting at, Auntie Fatima?

AUNTIE FATIMA The engagement is off, my son. As Noor is not here, could I ask you to collect the jewellery I gave her for the engagement? I especially want my mother's ring back.

ABDULLAH Auntie, please, do you know what this will do to Father? What this will do to Noor? She loves Rahman.

AUNTIE FATIMA I'm sorry, Abdullah, I've made up my mind.

ALI Auntie, let me talk to Rahman and explain the situation. I'm sure he'll understand.

AUNTIE FATIMA I'm sorry, Ali, *I've* made up my mind.

ABDULLAH Auntie, in the name of God the Merciful, the Compassionate, let me plead with you. Please reconsider ...

DAOUD You will destroy Noor and you will destroy us. Auntie, how can you?

AUNTIE FATIMA Me, destroy your family? Your father should not have been so permissive in allowing her to grow up so freely. That girl is too outspoken, always arguing with people. The neighbours always said that this girl will get in trouble sooner or later. You should have kept her at home so she would be a decent wife. How could you allow her to be exposed and violated by these savages?

DAOUD I will deal with these savages, but you have condemned Noor without hearing her.

AUNTIE FATIMA She condemned herself. I must do what is correct for my son. I have made up my mind.

ABDULLAH You are a mother, with a mother's heart. Noor is your child too.

AUNTIE FATIMA I am thinking of my son.

DAOUD And taking a knife to my sister's throat.

AUNTIE FATIMA Oh, don't be so dramatic, Daoud.

DAOUD Who will marry her now?

ABDULLAH Auntie, please, reconsider. Noor is your own child. I plead with you not to be hasty. Please, Auntie, let me get Father. Please talk to your older brother.

ALI Yes, Auntie, please talk to Father.

DAOUD Don't humiliate yourselves, brothers. This woman has no honour.

AUNTIE FATIMA I will not stay to be insulted in my brother's home! You can convey my decision to your father. I'm leaving now.(*Walks to the door.*) Don't forget my ring, Abdullah.

Auntie Fatima exits. The three brothers are in a state of shock, and sit silently.

DAOUD (*quietly, as though to himself*) Noor has been destroyed. It all goes back to the Crusaders. They are everywhere, destroying our lives.

FATHER (*entering the room*) What was all that noise? Did Noor come back? Has someone else come looking for her?

ABDULLAH Father, you should be resting.

FATHER I haven't been able to sleep. Every time I closed my eyes I saw Noor. I saw her sitting alone in her prison cell; she was calling out to me in anguish. I tried to run to her, but the iron bars were too strong. The guards found me and began beating me, I could feel their rifle butts in my stomach ... Was someone here? I thought I heard Auntie Fatima.

ALI Yes, it was Auntie Fatima.

FATHER But ... She did not ask to see me? My own sister did not come to greet me?

ALI She only came to –

FATHER I had forgotten about Rahman. The two must be so worried. I know Auntie Fatima loves Noor as a daughter.

DAOUD Father. Auntie Fatima came to bring us a message.

FATHER (*looks at Daoud quizzically*) What message?

DAOUD She has broken the engagement.

FATHER (*beginning to hyperventilate*) How can she do this?! Oh, my poor Noor! She has been dishonoured twice! She is lost, we are lost! How can I face my family and friends? This is too shameful for me to bear.

Father leans on his chair as though stricken. Abdullah

tries to hold him, but Father pushes him away, trying to get to the door.

FATHER Everything is falling apart. I will talk to Fatima, I will convince her ... yes, she is a good woman, she will understand. Ali, bring my coat.

Ali brings Father's coat.

ABDULLAH Father, in your condition you mustn't go out.

FATHER (*slowly*) I have to talk to Fatima.

ALI Then I'm going with you. You can't go alone.

ABDULLAH Yes, one of us must accompany you.

FATHER I'm capable of looking after myself! I'm not helpless.

ABDULLAH Please, Father, let Ali accompany you.

FATHER Let's go, then.

Father walks out slowly, accompanied by Ali. Daoud, seething with anger and clenching his fists, exits upstairs to his room. Abdullah slumps into his chair. After a while he takes the prayer mat and unfolds it on the floor. He bows his head on it and holds his palms together, looking towards Heaven and praying.

ABDULLAH O God, who hears the beggar's plea and the prince's prayer, who never turns away those who are in pain and in need. O God, You who guided Abraham's knife away from his son's throat; who spoke to Moses on Mount Sinai; who gave Jesus the power to bring the dead back to life; You, who revealed the mysteries of Heaven to our beloved Muhammad on that miraculous night journey; God of my fathers and forefathers; Merciful God, who never turns away those who seek You, listen to the prayer of this sinner.

Abdullah wipes tears from his eyes and sits on the mat for a while. Daoud enters.

ABDULLAH I've just said a prayer for Noor. Are you going to meet with Imam Khaliq again?

Daoud is unresponsive, lost in thought.

ABDULLAH Daoud?

DAOUD Hmm? Oh ... I ... yes. I will be leaving soon. I have another appointment.

ABDULLAH I will be anxious to know the result.

They are silent

ABDULLAH When will you return?

DAOUD I am not sure.

ABDULLAH Oh, Daoud, you wear your heart on your sleeve. (*Pauses.*) You haven't changed. Do you remember when you were eleven, you got into that huge fist-fight with that boy at school?

DAOUD I was twelve.

ABDULLAH You told me before you left that you were going to make him pay. You were so angry at that boy – Tariq – for ... what was he doing?

DAOUD He had pinned down Karim and forced a lighted cigarette in his mouth. He was doing things like that all the time.

ABDULLAH I remember.

DAOUD (*shakes his head*) I *was* really angry at him ... it wasn't right, it wasn't fair. I hate bullies. He got away with everything; no one would stand up to him.

ABDULLAH (*almost laughing*) That's exactly what you said then. That he wasn't going to get away with it, that his strength meant nothing to you.

Pauses.

You looked the same as you do now: determined. I

see you; I know when you are planning something. I 'm afraid, Daoud. I'm afraid for you, for all of us.

DAOUD Brother, you are just imagining things. Leave everything to God. God is the Just, and the Avenger.

ABDULLAH Stop talking of vengeance. Noor will be returned to us, *insh'allah*. We should have faith.

DAOUD I do have faith. *Insh'allah*, honour will be redeemed.

ABDULLAH Daoud, I know you think I am some hopeless mystic lost in my own world and out of tune with the times, but I am not blind. I see you have darkened your eyes, trimmed your beard and put on white clothes. I see your calm demeanour and collected appearance, as if some great weight has been lifted off your shoulders.

DAOUD You are just imagining things.

ABDULLAH I see a warrior ready to be greeted by the *houris* in Paradise.

DAOUD (*slowly*) The will of God will be done.

ABDULLAH It is up to us to translate the will of God. You yourself told me how you have always argued against violence, even facing the firebrands in your 'network'. What has made you change your mind now?

DAOUD If you don't understand, then you don't know me at all. I have spent hours struggling with myself ever since Noor was taken, and even then I remained undecided. But when her engagement was broken ... I had no more doubt.

ABDULLAH Nothing has changed, Daoud – nothing. I know you. Violence didn't work then, and it won't work now. Did Tariq change his ways because you fought him? No, he didn't stop tormenting Karim until Ali told your teacher what was going on, and even showed him the cigarettes Tariq kept in his pocket.

DAOUD Ali? What has he done *now* to get her back, besides crawl on his belly to that fat, corrupt, money-grubbing minister? Did you see how he acted with the soldiers? He wouldn't even look up, that's how frightened he was. He's become so spineless.

ABDULLAH As a faithful Muslim, you should be kinder to him.

DAOUD Why does he need kindness? He wasn't in jail for long. Our own sister has been there longer.

ABDULLAH For someone like Ali, a few hours in prison is like a few years. You have no idea what happened to him in prison, the violation that *he* experienced.

DAOUD (*interest piqued*) What did they do to him? What did they do to my brother?

ABDULLAH The words would barely come out of his mouth, that's how frightened and traumatised he was. I can't even repeat it, it's too awful.

DAOUD So they *did* torture him?

He lets the reality sink in; his tone becomes repentant.

God have mercy on us all ...

ABDULLAH I fear his soul has suffered the most. He is still holding onto his ideals of right and wrong, even though he has seen with his own eyes that they don't exist, not in this country anyway. I fear his denial will drive him crazy, and maybe it has already affected him.

DAOUD I'm so sorry. I had no idea. I didn't think to ask ... I have been too hard, too harsh, with him.

ABDULLAH These are terrible times. The only salvation is in holding onto the idea and practice of compassion. I am not sure what you are planning, but whatever it is, think of us. Think of Noor.

DAOUD I *am* thinking of my sister. I am thinking of all my sisters. And all my brothers.

ABDULLAH Daoud ...

DAOUD No, brother, please. I respect you, but now you must listen to me. You must hear me. I have been searching my heart for the last few days. I have not been able to sleep. I look around me, and I see so much pain, and I wonder whether my work is making any difference at all. I hurt and bleed like anyone else. I have just lost the two women who have been the closest to me in my life. My medicine not only failed to ease Mother's pain, but it failed me as well. Even my prayers went unanswered. I can still see her face in every patient that I treat. Now with Noor, I am being tested yet again. I am human, Abdullah.

ABDULLAH Yes, Daoud, you are human. But that is not enough. We must be better than human if we are to change anything.

DAOUD I intend to do so.

ABDULLAH I am not sure whether we are understanding one another. I can only imagine what you are going to do, so please think the matter through.

DAOUD I have.

ABDULLAH I don't know what to say. You no longer respect my opinion.

DAOUD Brother, I have always respected you. You must respect *my* decision. I shall be leaving shortly, as soon my car arrives. Take care of Father, and especially take care of Noor.

ABDULLAH Well, she needs *you*. We all need you ... and your fiancée needs you.

DAOUD Zeinab is not yet my fiancée.

Sighs.

We have argued about this so many times, brother. You keep acting like I don't know what love is. I do. But the tyrants who are poisoning our lives know nothing of love. They only understand the language of violence. An eye for an eye ... it's in their Bible.

The sound of a car pulling up outside is followed by a voice. Daoud becomes jumpy and rushes to open the door.

DAOUD My ride is here.

Daoud returns to embrace Abdullah, who is bewildered.

DAOUD *Assalaam alaikum*. God keep you in His protection, brother.

Fadel enters, followed by Noor. Daoud and Abdullah gasp, completely taken aback.

ABDULLAH Praise be to God! Noor has returned!

DAOUD Noor.

ABDULLAH God has heard my prayers! He is truly the Compassionate, the Merciful!

DAOUD (*addressing Fadel*) Welcome, brother.

FADEL I was driving home past the prison when I saw this young girl all by herself on the highway, looking lost.

ABDULLAH Thank you, my brother, thank you on behalf of our family! God be praised, Noor is back!

Abdullah runs up to Noor, hugs her and kisses her on the forehead.

ABDULLAH God is Merciful.

DAOUD Sister, are you all right? What happened? How did you get here? Are you hurt ...?

NOOR I'm fine, brothers, I'm home now. This gentleman has been very kind to me. I –

Noor falters and almost faints into Daoud's arms.

ABDULLAH Quickly, we must get her off her feet.

Abdullah and Daoud take Noor to the recliner, where she stretches out, her eyes half-closed.

DAOUD Noor. Can you hear me? *(To Abdullah)* Get some water immediately. You see what they did to my sister? Do you think I will ever tolerate this?

ABDULLAH (*goes to the kitchen*) Daoud, tend to her.

FADEL I know what they do in those prisons. She's been starved of sleep and malnourished for God knows how long, I can see it in her eyes.

DAOUD And you sir, are ...?

FADEL My name is Fadel. I'm only a truck driver, but I, too, have had relatives taken to the Holiday Inn. The guards don't even allow prisoners to make one phone call. They release the prisoners without any notice and throw them out into the street. It was early in the morning, and this is not a good time for a young girl to be on her own. So I stopped and asked if I could help.

DAOUD Brother, you have been a true Muslim.

ABDULLAH (*returning and bringing a glass of water to Noor's mouth*) Come on ... slowly now ...

NOOR (*regains her senses, pushes Abdullah's arm away*) No, I am fasting.

DAOUD (*kissing her proudly on the forehead*) *Mash'allah*. Of course you are; you are a virtuous Muslim.

ABDULLAH (*to Fadel*) How can we repay you for your kindness? Can we compensate you in any way? At least let me serve you tea or food.

FADEL Thank you, but I'm fasting. No, please, don't talk about compensation. It was my duty. This girl's honour is the honour of every man in this land. I have a daughter too, and I worry when I have to leave her alone.

ABDULLAH (*moving forward to embrace him*) We have no words to thank you.

FADEL Praise is for God. It is a miracle your sister is out. God filled the heart of someone high up with mercy. She must have the blessings of her elders.

ABDULLAH God is truly great.

FADEL She's safe, and I leave her in your hands. I must now return to my family. *Assalaam alaikum.*

DAOUD & ABDULLAH *Wa alaikum assalaam.*

Fadel exits. Noor recovers some more and looks around.

NOOR Has he left already? I didn't get a chance to thank him again.

Tries to get up, but quickly falls back into the recliner.

Where is Father? How is Ali?

ABDULLAH Noor, you mustn't strain yourself. You must rest.

Heads towards the TV set.

Shall I put this on?

NOOR Oh no, I am fine ...

DAOUD Noor, tell me, how do you feel?

NOOR (*speaking slowly and as though far away, in a daze*) I'm just tired. It's so cold in here. Where is Father? I've been worried ... Has he been taking his medicine?

Where is Ali? Is he still in that horrible place? I don't know what happened to him ...

ABDULLAH Ali came back yesterday, safe and sound. They just scared him a little. He left earlier with Father to look for you.

NOOR I was so worried that Ali would be shaken out of his wits by those cruel people. He is always such a stickler for what is right and wrong.

ABDULLAH Are you sure you don't want anything to eat or drink?

NOOR Yes, I'm sure.

DAOUD She has already said she is fasting. Don't badger her about it. Did they hurt you, Noor? Were you ... harmed?

ABDULLAH Daoud!

NOOR I kept repeating all of your favourite Qur'anic verses, Daoud. I closed my eyes and imagined Mother was there with me, holding my hand, telling me everything would be alright, to be brave. She was so beautiful. There was a shining light pouring from her face.

DAOUD Noor. My little sister.

NOOR Where is her picture? I want to hold it for a little while.

Abdullah hands Noor the photo.

NOOR Oh, the glass is broken ... no matter, I can still see her. She's smiling at me, can you see her smile? How did this break?

ABDULLAH Noor, I'm going to order some tasty dishes of lamb *pilaf* for *iftar*. Anything else I should order?

NOOR Any vegetable dish will do.

ABDULLAH I am sorry, I had forgotten you stopped eating meat.

I should have remembered Daoud teasing you about having become a Hindu. I will make sure we have vegetarian dishes.

NOOR You have all already forgotten about me, it seems.

DAOUD We never stopped thinking about you for a moment.

NOOR I saw your face too, brother Abdullah. You were there with your prayer beads, repeating the names of God ...

Smiling.

It was beautiful.

Pauses.

And Father ... Where is he? When will he be back?

ABDULLAH Let me see if I can locate Father and tell him the good news, he will be so thrilled.

Abdullah goes to the telephone and dials.

ABDULLAH Hello? Yes, hello? Can you please ask Mr Hussein to ring his house as soon as he arrives?

Pauses, listening.

I am Abdullah, his son. Just tell him: 'Noor is back safely.' This is urgent, please. Thank you.

DAOUD What happened to your glasses?

NOOR I lost them, but no matter, I think I still have my old pair upstairs.

DAOUD And the cut on your nose?

Noor doesn't seem to hear, and sighs.

ABDULLAH (*glaring at Daoud*) Father will be back, Noor, as soon as he gets my message.

NOOR I can't wait to see him.

DAOUD Noor. Were you ... Did they ... molest you?

ABDULLAH (*sharply*) Daoud, this is not the time!

NOOR The dogs didn't frighten me with their barking. I sang to myself, just as Mother used to sing to me, and they lay down in front of me. God softened their hearts.

DAOUD Are you feeling yourself?

NOOR I resolved that I would be strong and calm for all of you. I love you all so much. I am home now, and that is all that matters. How is Rahman? I thought about him too. He does worry so. And Auntie Fatima must be so concerned about me.

ABDULLAH Why don't you rest. We'll talk later, when Father returns. He has really missed you.

NOOR Daoud, can you get me a hot-water bottle? I feel tired and cold.

DAOUD Gladly.

Daoud speaks softly to Abdullah, out of Noor's hearing.

DAOUD I know she is in pain. She was tortured by those brutes. I promise you, I will avenge her.

ABDULLAH Nothing happened, Daoud, nothing *happened*. It's over; God has protected Noor. She is home, and she is safe now.

Offers Daoud the phone.

Here. You can call your contacts and tell them your plans are no longer required.

DAOUD You just don't understand, brother.

ABDULLAH But Noor is back. It's over.

DAOUD It is wonderful that Noor has been returned to us, but our honour has already been violated all the same. I've made up my mind. I have to strike back for Noor, for what they did to Ali, for the honour of our people.

ABDULLAH Please, Daoud, *please.* I implore you, God has been merciful, He has brought back Noor safely. Ali has returned. Father will be home shortly. Everything will be as it was.

DAOUD Noor is *not* back safely. I am a medical doctor, and I can tell. She is in pain. She is just putting on a brave act.

ABDULLAH Violence will not heal Noor. You are going to put all our lives in danger. You don't think things through.

DAOUD I have in this case, and I will not be swayed from my path. I can't wait for my ride any longer. I must leave now.

Daoud crosses back to Noor.

DAOUD Noor, I'm going out now. Everything will be alright.

NOOR You're leaving already? I've so much to talk to you about.

DAOUD I have to attend to something urgently.

NOOR When will you return?

DAOUD It may be a while.

NOOR Where are you going?

DAOUD I have a mission to perform.

NOOR Is your mission more important than me?

DAOUD It is about you, my little darling sister.

NOOR (*sitting up, clearly alarmed*) Daoud, my brother, my dear, dear brother, what are you planning? I have a bad feeling about this.

DAOUD Whatever I am going to do will reflect my love for you, Noor.

NOOR (*newly energised*) But why are you leaving? You still love me, don't you? I'm still your sister!

DAOUD Of course I love you, Noor ... that's why I'm going. They have dishonoured you ...

NOOR (*beginning to hyperventilate*) Daoud, you keep talking of honour. I am still honourable! My honour has not been compromised!

DAOUD But, Noor ...

Abdullah quietly moves back to allow Daoud and Noor space, staying out of the conversation.

NOOR Do you want a doctor to examine me? Don't you believe me? I am pure. Whole. They ... could not break my spirit. You and I, Daoud, must hold firm so that we can rebuild this country with justice and compassion.

DAOUD These are evil people and they will be punished, *insh'allah*.

NOOR However evil they are, God's mercy is greater, as they could not take my honour, my integrity. My life is not over, Daoud. Whatever you are planning, please, please, don't do it. Sit and talk to me, Daoud.

DAOUD I must leave ...

NOOR Do you remember when Mother died and I fell ill with pneumonia? I was so miserable. I thought I would die. Late at night, you came to my bedside and promised me that you would never let me feel the loss of a mother's love.

DAOUD (*hesitates, and sits down*) Yes, I ...

NOOR (*taking Daoud's hand tenderly*) Your love and protection took away the ache in my heart for Mother's loss. You fought with Auntie Fatima when she demanded I stop my college education and get married straightaway. You even helped me with my first college article. You told me of the rights Islam gives women. You are my brother and my friend and my champion.

DAOUD I did no more than any brother would have done, and you have always been special to me.

NOOR I constantly ask myself: what would the great Muslim role models have done today, the women of our beloved Prophet's household? They would have fought – but in a way the Prophet taught them. Through education, commitment and patience. Do you think they would be scared of barking dogs and some stupid ignorant men?

DAOUD I accept that, but ...

NOOR Let them take me to prison a thousand times. Let them torture me every time. I will never give up my dreams. I will never surrender my future. I want to fight for a society where girls are safe when they are on their way to and from school, where a citizen has justice and is not summarily dismissed after serving the government for decades, like Father; and where honour is defined to mean something more than the suppression of women.

DAOUD That is fine, and no one can disagree with it. But you must respect my way.

NOOR I do. But our ways are tied together. What you do will affect me and what I do will affect you. Why do you want to jeopardise everything? Our very future ...

DAOUD I don't ...

NOOR You have so much to give to our community, and I have so much to learn from you, to serve the poor and heal the sick. Without you, who will complete our favourite project? Think of what will happen to the *Islamia* school. Who will teach the little children in our neighbourhood then?

DAOUD I am sure God will look after them.

NOOR Yes, He will, Daoud, but He needs you here on Earth to help. Anger and violence are not the answer. I learned this lesson in prison. I cannot see you throwing your life away.

The telephone rings. Abdullah answers it discreetly and speaks into it.

ABDULLAH Yes, yes, it is true. She is with us now. I will tell her.

Turns to Noor and Daoud.

That was Ali. Father knows you are here, and is on his way.

DAOUD (*sits up with a start*) Then I must go!

NOOR No, Daoud. Wait for Father.

DAOUD (*stands up abruptly*) I cannot bear facing him.

NOOR Daoud, listen to me ...

ABDULLAH Noor is right. You have work to do. True Islamic work. She has come back, Daoud, and she doesn't want you to go. Doesn't that mean anything to you?

DAOUD (*moving to the door*) You cannot ask me to let them take the only thing we have left! God is great. God is great.

ABDULLAH This is not the way. I forbid you to leave. Daoud, talk to me.

Daoud opens the door, but hesitates at his brother's words.

DAOUD (*looking back*) The time for talking is over.

Daoud moves to exit.

NOOR (*rises to go after him*) Daoud! Daoud, don't go.

ABDULLAH (*moves towards the door after Daoud*) No, Daoud, stop.

Abdullah steps in front of Daoud, who pushes him aside.

DAOUD Don't stop me.

NOOR Daoud, don't.

ABDULLAH Stop!

The brothers scuffle.

NOOR Daoud!

DAOUD No one can stop me!

Daoud pushes Abdullah, who stumbles against the recliner. Daoud exits, slamming the door.

ABDULLAH He doesn't respect me anymore.

Abdullah is shaking, close to tears. Noor goes to him and helps him up.

NOOR He is so stubborn. It is impossible to talk to him when he's like that.

ABDULLAH This is not who we are. This is not Islam. We must not become like those we hate.

Noor seems lost for a moment, then falters and sits on the edge of the recliner.

NOOR He didn't even listen to me.

ABDULLAH Daoud is so frustrating. So obstinate. But for a moment I thought you had changed his mind.

NOOR He is confused, but his heart is good.

ABDULLAH (*slumps dejectedly*) It seems I have found my sister, but lost a brother.

NOOR (*putting her hands on Abdullah's shoulders reassuringly*)

No, you will not, brother. I promise you. I am going after Daoud as soon as I have seen Father and assured him that I am well.

ABDULLAH Where will you look?

NOOR I have a good idea. Daoud is so easy to read.

ABDULLAH (*straightening up*) Will you prevail?

NOOR Noor will prevail. I have learned that from you, brother.

Gentle flute music plays, fading into the background once Noor begins speaking. Noor and Father are now upstairs in Father's room. The scene is calm. Father is lying in bed, eyes closed, smiling and strangely serene. A single candle burns by his bedside – the electricity is off again. Noor sits in a chair near the head of the bed, holding a book. She recites a poem without looking at it. She sounds calm and self-assured.

NOOR (*reading*) Out beyond ideas of wrong-doing and right-doing there is a field, I shall meet you there

Noor stops, and then resumes, slowly.

When the soul lies down in that grass
The world is too full to talk about
This moment thine
This love comes to rest in me
In one wheat grain a thousand sheave stacks
Inside
The needle's eye
A turning night of stars.
Out beyond ideas of wrong-doing and right-doing
there is a field,
I shall meet you there.

The lights fade.

THE TRIAL OF DARA SHIKOH

A Play in Three Acts

Dramatis Personae

Qazi Faizul Haq
Learned, dry scholar. Presides over the court. Mid-fifties. Bearded. Wears grand, flowing, green robes.

Dara Shikoh
Eldest son of Emperor Shah Jehan, who has declared him Crown Prince. Early forties. Slim, elegant, poetic and impractical; a passionate scholar of mysticism. Fighting a losing battle for his beliefs of universal acceptance and compassion in a world in which he appears lost. Appears wearing torn and dirty but once-elegant clothes, looking tired and unshaven.

Prosecutor Abdullah Khan
Plodding, plotting bureaucrat. Mid-forties. Eager to please the new dispensation forming around him in Delhi.

Attendant 1:
To the *qazi* in court, wears more refined and elegant clothes than others in the courtroom.

Attendant 2
To the Emperor, wears more refined and elegant clothes than others in the courtroom.

Gopi Lal
First witness. Hindu mystic and scholar dressed in saffron robes. Face and head are shaven. Bears the marks of a religious Hindu.

Bahadur Singh
Second witness. Sikh religious leader. Wears turban and traditional white *shalwar kameez*. Fully bearded.

Courtroom Attendees
Young Muslim men wearing traditional clothes.

Aurangzeb
Younger brother of Dara Shikoh, now self-declared Emperor of the Mughal Empire. Late thirties. Serious and sober; takes his work as champion of Islam to be his destiny. Passionate in his defence of Islam, believing he is on a mission to save it from internal and external attack. He appears simply dressed in the first scene.

Jahanara
Wise, compassionate elder sister of Dara and Aurangzeb. Also a mystic scholar, and a humanist. Can see each brother's points of view, but her interest is in preserving the integrity of the family and therefore the dynasty. Simply dressed.

Roshanara
Younger, passionate sister of Dara and Aurangzeb; identifies strongly with the latter's version of Islamic culture and politics.

Sipihr
Dara Shikoh's confused teenage son, unsure of what is happening around him.

Guard
Wears the royal tunic of the Imperial Guard: headdress, satin saffron-coloured shirt with close collar and yellow sash; carries sword and lantern.

Hakim Bukhari
Court physician. Has long, white beard. Tired, stooped in appearance. Wears expensive clothes.

Jahanara's Attendant
Young, solicitous woman.

ACT I

Courtroom. Delhi, August 1659. Dara Shikoh stands accused of apostasy. Qazi Faizul Haq presides.

QAZI FAIZUL HAQ Let the trial of the accused, Prince Dara Shikoh, begin. Please present the evidence on behalf of the prosecution first. We will hear who will represent the accused.

DARA SHIKOH I will, Your Honour.

QAZI FAIZUL HAQ Are you sure? We can provide a good defence counsel for you.

DARA SHIKOH No. I am ready to confront my accusers.

QAZI FAIZUL HAQ Please proceed, then. Are there witnesses in this case?

PROSECUTOR KHAN I have here, o wise and noble Qazi, three witnesses to help establish my case, and I am sure the accused will not object.

QAZI FAIZUL HAQ (*making notes*) And who are these witnesses?

PROSECUTOR KHAN The first prosecution witness is the Hindu scholar Gopi Lal; the second is the Sikh religious scholar Bahadur Singh.

QAZI FAIZUL HAQ You said 'three witnesses'.

PROSECUTOR KHAN The third is the accused himself.

QAZI FAIZUL HAQ That is interesting. So you will both be sharing the witnesses. This will make for an unusual case.

PROSECUTOR KHAN I would like to examine my witnesses, calling Dara Shikoh last.

QAZI FAIZUL HAQ *Prince* Dara Shikoh, Abdullah Khan, *Prince* Dara Shikoh. This court will uphold the honour of the defendant by referring to the correct title given him by birth.

PROSECUTOR KHAN I am sorry. You are right. 'Prince Dara Shikoh', it is. I request permission, Your Honour, to summon my first witness, the Hindu scholar Gopi Lal.

QAZI FAIZUL HAQ Summon the witness.

ATTENDANT I Gopi Lal, please present yourself in the witness box.

Gopi Lal walks up to the witness box. The attendant brings out a copy of the Hindu holy scriptures and presents it to him.

QAZI FAIZUL HAQ Please swear on your holy scriptures that you will tell the truth and nothing but the truth.

GOPI LAL I swear to tell nothing but the truth.

PROSECUTOR KHAN To the best of your knowledge, is it true that Prince Dara personally oversaw the translation of the Hindu holy texts, *The Upanishads*, from Sanskrit into Persian for the first time? And *The Bhagavad Gita* as well?

GOPI LAL Yes, it is.

PROSECUTOR KHAN Is it true that Prince Dara called *The Upanishads* 'God's most perfect revelation'?

GOPI LAL That is true.

PROSECUTOR KHAN And is it true that Prince Dara claims there are veiled references to *The Upanishads* in the Holy Qur'an as the first heavenly book, the fountainhead and ocean of monotheism?

GOPI LAL This, too, is true. Our religious texts have illuminated the world since the dawn of history. We take pride in sharing the divine light with all of humanity.

PROSECUTOR KHAN And are these texts as sacred to Hindus as the holy Qur'an is to Muslims?

GOPI LAL Yes, sir.

PROSECUTOR KHAN So why was a Muslim chosen to perform this task of translation?

GOPI LAL There is a marvellous story that provides an explanation, sir. It was Lord Ram himself who chose Prince Dara for this noble task.

PROSECUTOR KHAN I am sorry, I do not understand. Could you please explain this so that a simple Muslim like me can understand?

GOPI LAL Lord Ram appeared in a dream to Prince Dara Shikoh. He commanded the Prince to have these ancient sacred texts translated into Persian, so that the world would discover their wisdom and beauty.

PROSECUTOR KHAN Please note, Your Honour, that it was the Hindu god Ram who asked the accused in a dream to translate these Hindu texts. Please note, Hindu gods do not appear to normal Muslims, and certainly not to provide instruction to them to propagate alien ideologies. You will have noted, Your Honour, that the accused has attempted to establish Hinduism as a monotheistic religion that even predates Islam and, indeed, the other Abrahamic faiths. This is nothing but blasphemy. Thank you, Gopi Lal. No more questions.

Gopi Lal leaves the witness box.

PROSECUTOR KHAN May I call the Sikh scholar Bahadur Singh, Your Honour?

QAZI FAIZUL HAQ Summon the witness.

ATTENDANT 1 Bahadur Singh, please present yourself in the witness box.

Bahadur Singh walks up to the witness box. Attendant 1 brings out a copy of the Sikh holy scriptures and presents it to him.

QAZI FAIZUL HAQ Please swear on your holy scriptures that you will tell the truth and nothing but the truth.

BAHADUR SINGH I swear to tell nothing but the truth.

PROSECUTOR KHAN Bahadur Singh, for the enlightenment of the court, could you explain the Sikh doctrine?

QAZI FAIZUL HAQ I think we are all familiar with the Sikh religion.

PROSECUTOR KHAN Your Honour, I am, of course, a scholar of religions and therefore familiar with the Sikh religion; but I wish to establish the credentials of the witness. After all, we want a credible Sikh scholar to give testimony.

QAZI FAIZUL HAQ Proceed, then.

BAHADUR SINGH The Sikh faith is born of the soil of India, and in it we can see the reflection of the two great religions of the land, Islam and Hinduism. The Sikhs mirror the best of both religions, and are therefore a natural bridge between the great religions of the world.

PROSECUTOR KHAN That is sufficient. In examining this witness, Your Honour, I will establish the blasphemous nature of Prince Dara's distortion of Islam. I am told, Bahadur Singh, that there are verses written by your Guru Nanak himself which equate the Hindu god Ram to Rahim.

Clearing throat conspicuously.

Ahem, I would like you to please note, Your Honour, that in these verses Ram has been equated to Rahim, which Your Honour recognises as another name for the God of Islam, the one true and Almighty God of creation.

BAHADUR SINGH Yes, there are some wonderful verses of the beloved Guruji that equate the two.

Strikes a theatrical pose and begins to recite in dramatic tones.

Ram, Rahim, Puran, Qur'an
Anek kahein, sab ek manyo.

Let me now translate this for those not fortunate enough to understand the beauty of the Punjabi language:

Whether we call Him Ram, or Rahim the Merciful,
or by myriad names
given in the Hindu Puranas and the Qur'an, we believe
Him to be One and
the Same.

PROSECUTOR KHAN Thank you, Bahadur Singh, for confirming your philosophy in which you equate Ram and Rahim. But tell me, are you suggesting that Muslims, Hindus, and Sikhs have at the core of their faiths similar beliefs and world-views?

BAHADUR SINGH Yes, *khan sahib*, I am. And I can do no better than to once again quote the verses of our honourable Guru. This is one of my favourites, as it goes to the roots of Sikh and Sufi self-discipline: the full acceptance of His will without complaint, and with courage. It is very, very stoic in its roots. In Punjabi we call it *bhanna manana* – accepting His Power and Will.

PROSECUTOR KHAN Could you get on with it, please? We do have other witnesses to examine.

BAHADUR SINGH Yes, yes. I am sorry; I do get carried away.

Kiv Sachayara hoiye?
Kiv kude tutte paal?
Hukam Rajai chalna,
Nanak likhya naal.

O, the music of my mother tongue. Let me translate:

How shall we know the Truth?

How can the veil of darkness or dust be rent asunder?
Walk in the path of His Will and Law,
which Nanak says are written within you.

PROSECUTOR KHAN Thank you, Bahadur Singh. I am sure you do your community proud in the way you recite these poems. Certainly, Your Honour, you would have noted the contents of this particular poem. To dispel any doubt, let me ask the witness what these verses mean to the ordinary person.

BAHADUR SINGH These verses are the core of Sikh and Sufi philosophy, which we share. After rejecting the other paths to Salvation – the path of total silence, the Tantric path of satiation of the senses, the babbling of incantations, spells and the meaningless recitation of scriptures – Guruji argues that only by following the categorical imperative that commands love for all creation, and is implanted in everyone by His Will – call it an educated and totally independent conscience – can we know the Truth or see the 'Face of God'.

PROSECUTOR KHAN I am merely a simple believer, Your Honour. I confess I do not understand some of this language. But I do know that there is one truth that I was taught: the finality and superiority of Islam. By suggesting that we can discover the 'Truth' or the 'Face of God' through paths other than Islam, I am certain we are *deviating* from Islam. Indeed, Your Honour, I maintain that we have established through the verses of the founder of the Sikh faith the exact nature of this deviation from the true beliefs of Islam. Please note that I intend to prove that Prince Dara Shikoh shares these beliefs. It is precisely for this reason that the Sikhs favour Prince Dara Shikoh.

BAHADUR SINGH Yes, indeed, we do favour him. He is truly a saintly man.

PROSECUTOR KHAN Is it true that when Prince Dara Shikoh fell gravely ill, your most holy religious leader, the Guru himself, prayed for his recovery?

BAHADUR SINGH It is true, sir. And the power of the Guru worked, and our Prince Dara recovered. We distributed sweets in celebration.

PROSECUTOR KHAN So you will agree that Prince Dara is seen as especially close to the Sikhs?

BAHADUR SINGH That is so, sir.

PROSECUTOR KHAN Would you explain to the court why Prince Dara is so beloved of the Sikhs?

BAHADUR SINGH There is a deep bond between Prince Dara Shikoh and the Sikhs. Prince Dara is a disciple of Mian Mir, the Sufi saint of Lahore; and it was Mian Mir whom we Sikhs requested to lay the foundation stone of our Golden Temple in Amritsar. He did, and has thus entered the heart of every Sikh. Yes, sir, Prince Dara is beloved among the Sikhs.

PROSECUTOR KHAN Thank you, Bahadur Singh. That will be all.

Bahadur Singh leaves the witness box.

PROSECUTOR KHAN I would now like to officially examine my third witness: Prince Dara Shikoh.

QAZI FAIZUL HAQ The third witness may take the stand.

Dara Shikoh walks to the witness box and is handed a copy of the Qur'an by Attendant 1.

DARA SHIKOH (*placing his hand on the Qur'an*) I swear to tell nothing but the truth.

PROSECUTOR KHAN I have here two documents with which to begin the examination of my final witness and to establish a clear-cut case of apostasy. Would the accused verify that he is the author of *The Mingling of the Oceans* and *The Great Secret*?

DARA SHIKOH Yes, I am the author of both.

PROSECUTOR KHAN Could you explain, as a favour to the court, what you mean by the titles of these two documents? What 'oceans' are you referring to in the first title, and what is this 'great secret'?

DARA SHIKOH Both contain my philosophy, which I have developed all my life in order to discover the common sources of our spiritual being, that which transcends particularistic faith and elevates us to the knowledge of the Unknowable and the Unseen.

PROSECUTOR KHAN Could you translate that in simple language? Language that someone simple, like me, can understand?

DARA SHIKOH I think I have been as plain as I can be. The matter is quite clear.

PROSECUTOR KHAN Let me then attempt to clarify what I have understood from reading these two works. Is it correct to say that the main idea in the books is to convey the common source, common bonds and, indeed, common character of Islam and Hinduism? That, in their essence, they are similar – one and the same?

DARA SHIKOH In essence, yes.

A gasp goes up in the courtroom.

QAZI FAIZUL HAQ Silence! I will hear this case with respect to the court. I will not have emotional outbursts.

PROSECUTOR KHAN So the noble monotheism of Islam, preached by the Prophet of Islam, peace be upon him, and the declaration of faith itself – 'There is no God but Allah, and Muhammad is his messenger' – is nullified by you. Moreover, it is equated to the polytheism preached in Hinduism, with its many gods taking many diverse shapes.

DARA SHIKOH In essence, yes. The driving force and overarching idea behind both are the same. Islam and Hinduism meet at the source, and there is much in common. Of course, their history, their rituals and even their forms are different. The aim of a great religion like Islam, or indeed Hinduism, is to produce pious, compassionate, and concerned individuals.

PROSECUTOR KHAN Are you suggesting that Muslims should allow other religions to flourish?

DARA SHIKOH As a Muslim, you *must* allow other religions to flourish.

PROSECUTOR KHAN You'll note, o wise Qazi, that Prince Dara Shikoh is already admitting to a deviation from Islam.

DARA SHIKOH Not at all. I am simply reflecting the core philosophy of Islam. The Qur'an categorically states: 'There is no compulsion in religion.' This is as final a statement as you can ever get to define religion.

PROSECUTOR KHAN (*looking through his papers*) I have here a phrase attributed to you ... yes, here it is. In this document, you have written a phrase that reads: 'Love alone is the Ultimate Truth, the rest is ritual.' Did you write this? And if so, what do you mean by it?

DARA SHIKOH The phrase should be self-evident. We are faced with our nature, which is dominated by anger, hatred and jealousy. But we also possess the antidote to these terrible human emotions, and the antidote reflects the divine part of our nature – and that is love. If we can develop this attribute of the divine, we can overcome our base nature. Thus, love is the Ultimate Truth, and the Ultimate Reality.

PROSECUTOR KHAN And what would you do with rituals like the five daily prayers? Abolish them?

DARA SHIKOH No, not at all. Don't trivialise the deep human impulse to discover the path to God through worship. That, too, is what the Qur'an teaches us. Prayer helps us to love; in no case does it hinder or prevent us from reaching out to others.

First and Second Courtroom Attendees mutter in appreciation.

COURT ATTENDEE 1 Subhanallah.

COURT ATTENDEE 2 Beautiful answer.

PROSECUTOR KHAN No one is denying the glory of Islam and its enlightened principles. Let me turn to another writing by the accused. I have here a poem written by the accused, titled *What shall I do?* Let me first confirm whether the accused accepts authorship of this poem. Did you, Prince Dara Shikoh, write this poem with the following words: *I know not what I am / I am not a Christian / I am neither Jew / nor Gabonese nor a Muslim?*

DARA SHIKOH I did. Yes, those are my verses.

PROSECUTOR KHAN 'I am not a Muslim': the words of the accused, Your Honour, in which he unequivocally rejects Islam. There is nothing further left for me to add. The accused has accepted his crime. He has rejected Islam from his own mouth, and I ask the court to pronounce the punishment for apostasy according to Islamic law.

QAZI FAIZUL HAQ What have you to say in your defence, Prince Dara Shikoh? Do you accept that these are your verses?

DARA SHIKOH I have said what I have to say, and yes, these are my verses. If I am guilty, then so are Islam's most celebrated mystic poets, Maulana Rumi and Sheikh Ibn Arabi. I am in good company, and I will happily go to join them.

PROSECUTOR KHAN Let me develop the theme of the poem by the accused. Prince Dara Shikoh, you are so close to the Sikhs that you are beloved by them. We just heard confirmation of this sentiment from the Sikh scholar, Bahadur Singh. Yet you call yourself a Muslim. Is it not true that Islam categorically declares that the final messenger of God was our beloved prophet?

DARA SHIKOH That is certainly true, and I have never denied it.

PROSECUTOR KHAN Then if our beloved Prophet is the final messenger, how can you accept these other messengers the Sikhs call 'Gurus'? Did they not claim to bring the word of God a thousand years after our holy Prophet?

DARA SHIKOH Islam believes that God has sent 124,000 messengers and sages to remind us of the right path. They have been sent by God to different peoples in different lands to speak in different languages. Great religious teachers have continued to articulate the transcendent values of the Divine up to our own times. I am sure that Guru Nanak is such a figure. He is a true spiritual teacher whose wisdom embraces everyone. Guru Nanak –

PROSECUTOR KHAN The same Guru Nanak who insulted all scholars of Islam? The Guru Nanak who especially targeted the true guardians of the state, the *qazis*? I would like the court, o Honourable Qazi, to note what Guru Nanak said about *qazis*: 'The *qazis* who sit in the courts to minister justice, rosary in hand and the name of God on their lips, commit *injustice* if their palms are not greased. And if someone challenges them, lo, they quote the scriptures.'

COURT ATTENDEE 1 Shame!

COURT ATTENDEE 2 This is an insult to Islam!

QAZI FAIZUL HAQ I have noted carefully these defamatory references to the *qazis* of Islam.

PROSECUTOR KHAN Now let me establish a link between the thought of Guru Nanak and the accused. This is what Prince

Dara Shikoh said: 'Paradise is there where there is no *mullah*.'

DARA SHIKOH I –

PROSECUTOR KHAN Unless he denies it now ...

QAZI FAIZUL HAQ Do you deny you said this?

DARA SHIKOH No, I don't. Both Guru Nanak and I meant that –

PROSECUTOR KHAN Please note that the accused, through his own mouth, has equated his ideas to those of Guru Nanak – the same Guru Nanak who made these hostile remarks about Islam.

DARA SHIKOH I object. Neither Guru Nanak nor I have ever made negative remarks about Islam. On the contrary. What both of us have done is to underline the spirituality of Islam, and to contrast it with the hypocrisy of its religious clerics who do not practise what they preach.

PROSECUTOR KHAN In short, you endorse Guru Nanak's vilification of all *qazis*.

QAZI FAIZUL HAQ Yes, I would like to know your answer to this question.

DARA SHIKOH I simply emphasise the inner spirituality of faith, and not its outward superficial behaviour, which can so easily degenerate into mechanical ritual and empty, hypocritical gestures.

PROSECUTOR KHAN The accused is just evading the question you asked, Your Honour. The accused has exposed himself.

DARA SHIKOH My Islam teaches me to understand and appreciate other societies and religions. That, too, is written in the Qur'an.

PROSECUTOR KHAN That is why the sort of Islam you practise encourages you to spend your time with non-believers, with so-called mystics, yogis and mendicants, like that

Sarmad. The Jew Sarmad wanders around like a beggar.

DARA SHIKOH Don't judge people by the simplicity or austerity of their appearance. Many a saint wears the clothes of a beggar, and I believe Sarmad is one such.

PROSECUTOR KHAN I am surprised at your friendship with Sarmad the Jew.

DARA SHIKOH Respect the wishes of Sarmad, as he has willingly accepted Islam; only God can judge what is in his heart, not you.

PROSECUTOR KHAN I suppose your friendship with Sarmad has nothing to do with the fact that he propagates your candidacy for the position of Emperor of the Mughal Empire.

DARA SHIKOH Sarmad's political opinions do not matter to me. I am interested in his spiritual insights.

PROSECUTOR KHAN I wonder how much he influences you about the strange practices of Sufism.

DARA SHIKOH The Qur'an teaches us to respect other faiths, so that in turn people can respect ours.

PROSECUTOR KHAN Is it written in the Qur'an to worship trees and rivers, as the Hindus do? And we have on record the words of Gopi Lal telling us that Lord Ram appears to you in your dreams.

DARA SHIKOH Both give life; therefore we must respect that which provides us sustenance.

PROSECUTOR KHAN And what about worshipping animals like the cow as divine?

DARA SHIKOH The cow helps us live better lives.

PROSECUTOR KHAN In what way, better lives? I am sure the Honourable Qazi would like to know.

DARA SHIKOH The cow provides us with milk and curds; its dung helps to cook food; its hide is used in many ways; and it assists the villagers in tilling the fields. Truly, the cow is like a mother that sustains us.

PROSECUTOR KHAN This is reducing everything to absurdity. Let me see how you will explain – and I hope you will not mind, Your Honour, but I need to ask this in order to pursue my case – the shameful obsession with the male and female sexual organs? There are entire cults and rituals around the *lingam* and the *yoni*.

DARA SHIKOH I appreciate that, expressed in this crude way, the subject could seem shocking; but in the abstract, they represent the unity of the male and the female. The *lingam* and the *yoni* represent the masculine and feminine in each individual. Together they create balance, thereby promoting enlightenment, bliss and worldly success.

PROSECUTOR KHAN Are you then suggesting that this is a different spirituality, a different truth?

DARA SHIKOH In answer, let me quote the *Rig Veda*: 'Truth is one; sages call it by various names.'

PROSECUTOR KHAN Perhaps your Lord Ram has inspired you to quote the *Rig Veda*. Please note, Your Honour, that Prince Dara Shikoh prefers to quote the Hindu text to the Qur'an.

DARA SHIKOH I have quoted the Qur'an in your courtroom several times this very day, Your Honour, and it reflects the same message of acceptance and openness as the Sikh and Hindu texts.

A gasp goes up in the courtroom.

QAZI FAIZUL HAQ I shall ignore the diversion, but shall request that emotions are kept under control in my courtroom! You may proceed.

PROSECUTOR KHAN I now wish to place before the court another piece of evidence to support my argument. For this purpose, may I ask the accused to extend his left hand towards the Honourable Qazi?

DARA SHIKOH I beg your pardon?

QAZI FAIZUL HAQ What is the purpose of this exercise?

PROSECUTOR KHAN I am merely building up my argument, Your Honour. So may I have Prince Dara Shikoh extend his left hand?

QAZI FAIZUL HAQ In the interest of establishing the facts of the case, I am sure Prince Dara will oblige.

DARA SHIKOH (*extending his left hand*) Is this what you want?

PROSECUTOR KHAN Thank you. Now, Your Honour, you will note that the accused has a large gold ring with ornate designs on it on his third finger.

QAZI FAIZUL HAQ Yes, I see it.

PROSECUTOR KHAN Is this your ring, Prince Dara?

DARA SHIKOH Yes, it is.

PROSECUTOR KHAN Would you tell the court: what is the origin of this ring? Where did you get it from?

DARA SHIKOH I had it designed and made myself.

PROSECUTOR KHAN May I request Prince Dara Shikoh to take off the ring and hand it to Your Honour for examination?

DARA SHIKOH (*gives ring to Qazi Faizul Haq*) Here is the ring.

QAZI FAIZUL HAQ (*examines the ring*) I don't see the point.

PROSECUTOR KHAN You will observe that there is an inscription on the ring.

QAZI FAIZUL HAQ Yes, I see it.

PROSECUTOR KHAN Now, if Your Honour would return the ring to the accused ...

QAZI FAIZUL HAQ (*returns the ring*) Would you clarify your line of argument?

PROSECUTOR KHAN I am coming to it, Your Honour. May I ask the accused to look at the ring and confirm that there is an inscription on it?

QAZI FAIZUL HAQ Yes, yes, we have established that fact. Get on with it. Prince Dara, please oblige.

DARA SHIKOH Yes, I confirm that there is writing on the ring.

PROSECUTOR KHAN Could you read the inscription on the ring aloud to the court?

DARA SHIKOH *Allah*. It says: *Allah*.

COURT ATTENDEE 1 *Alhamdulillah*.

COURT ATTENDEE 2 *Mash'allah*.

PROSECUTOR KHAN Now, could you please turn the ring round and read the other side?

DARA SHIKOH *Prabhu*.

PROSECUTOR KHAN *Prabhu*? And what does *Prabhu* mean?

DARA SHIKOH *Prabhu* is 'Master', 'Lord'; another name for God.

PROSECUTOR KHAN From which religious tradition does the name *Prabhu* derive? Is it Islamic?

DARA SHIKOH *Prabhu* is from the Hindu tradition. It is Sanskrit. No, it is not Islamic.

Softly uttered gasps are heard in the courtroom.

COURT ATTENDEE 1 *Astaghfirallah*!

COURT ATTENDEE 2 Sanskrit!

DARA SHIKOH *Allah* and *Prabhu*, Arabic and Sanskrit: the two universes are encompassed and counterpoised in harmony in one small ring. For me, the concept provides a visual representation in its continuum of the essence of our spiritual unity.

PROSECUTOR KHAN But what is the significance of these two names on one ring?

DARA SHIKOH I believe that God has different names. *Allah* and *Prabhu* are two of His names.

PROSECUTOR KHAN Are you suggesting that *Allah* and *Prabhu* are one and the same?

DARA SHIKOH I am merely expressing the need to open whichever of the doors each one of us has access to; these different doors lead us to the same reality, the –

PROSECUTOR KHAN *Allah* and *Prabhu*? One and the same? Even if the accused had the two names on two different rings on the same hand, it would have been blasphemous. But in this case, the two names are on the *same* ring, the two opposed and different concepts are fused and flow into each other.

QAZI FAIZUL HAQ I have noted your line of argument carefully.

PROSECUTOR KHAN You will also note, Your Honour, that the accused does not even deny his wrongdoing in equating *Allah* and *Prabhu*. What is worse, he is not even aware of his wrongdoing.

QAZI FAIZUL HAQ Have you finished with this line of argument?

PROSECUTOR KHAN Yes, Your Honour. Your Honour will also please note the accused has virtually admitted to equating a religion that worships snakes, stones and cows to the noble religion of Islam itself. He is admitting to having wandered from the straight path of Islam.

DARA SHIKOH You, sir, are an ignorant fool. The Mughal dynasty accepts and nurtures and appreciates all the different faiths that make up our great Empire. It is this that makes the Mughal dynasty different from the previous Muslim dynasties. It echoes the tradition of this great land. You would have heard of the Emperor

Ashoka, who in many ways was a forerunner of our own Akbar-e-Azam.

PROSECUTOR KHAN Precisely. That is why I need to remind the accused that we are proud to say that the Mughal Empire is an *Islamic* empire.

DARA SHIKOH And may I point to the strong respect the emperors have shown for other faiths. Emperor Akbar cited Jesus above all other religious figures on the main entrance of the *Buland Darwazah* of his new capital at Fatehpur Sikri. Even you, Abdullah Khan, would have seen the portraits of the Emperor Jahangir looking with deep devotional love at Mary, the mother of Jesus.

PROSECUTOR KHAN Well, I will concede that we do accept Christians as People of the Book. It is there in our Holy Qur'an; but that does not include the non-believers.

DARA SHIKOH Once again you have shown your ignorance of our own traditions. Babur, the founder of our dynasty, banned cow slaughter in Delhi as a mark of respect to our Hindu population. As for Akbar, there are so many examples. Akbar's chief wife was the Rajput princess Jodhabai, who was allowed to practise her culture and faith openly. Raja Toda Mal, who ran Akbar's administration so efficiently, was another prominent Hindu. As for the Sikhs, Akbar honoured them by presenting a gift of gold as a mark of respect to their holy book.

PROSECUTOR KHAN And would Prince Dara Shikoh tell the court what the leading Islamic cleric of his time thought of Akbar?

DARA SHIKOH Take care. You are referring to His Imperial Majesty Jalaluddin Muhammad Akbar, the Mughal-e-Azam. He is not plain 'Akbar'.

QAZI FAIZUL HAQ Yes. Decorum must be observed, and the due titles of this land honoured.

PROSECUTOR KHAN: I am sorry, Your Honour. Could the accused comment on what the leading cleric thought of the Mughal-e-Azam, Akbar?

DARA SHIKOH: The narrow-minded and the bigoted opposed Emperor Akbar, but they never discouraged him from uniting the land. This particular *mullah*, Ahmad Sirhindi –

PROSECUTOR KHAN: Point of order, Your Honour. Sheikh Ahmad Sirhindi needs to be referred to by his official title, Mujaddid Alf-e-Sani. Surely the most distinguished Islamic scholar of the Mughal Empire deserves the same respect as others in this court in the usage of titles – although the Sheikh may not have the privilege of royal birth ...

QAZI FAIZUL HAQ: Yes. We must observe correct decorum in court. This needs to be noted by all concerned.

DARA SHIKOH: Noted, Your Honour. Sheikh Mujaddid Alf-e-Sani finally accepted Imperial authority, and that is the point I wish to make. Some would call it compromise, and some would see it as his finding the correct path.

PROSECUTOR KHAN: The accused is again obfuscating the facts. The great Sheikh fought against the unorthodox accretions to Islam that came from the so-called mystics and Sufis. These people even challenged the concept of the unity of God Almighty, the central feature of Islam. God sent the great Sheikh to reinvigorate the faith of Islam, and when the Emperor Jahangir accepted the Sheikh's views, he was prepared to come out of prison. Under the Sheikh's supervision the Emperor Jahangir then removed everything that was contrary to Islam. In our case, before your court, Your Honour, it appears that the accused is speaking as though neither the Sheikh nor his reforms ever existed.

DARA SHIKOH: I believe that when the Sheikh was locked up in

Gwalior Fort it persuaded him to see the world differently, and he soon repented. He was lucky, for Gwalior is known as the 'destination of the damned'.

PROSECUTOR KHAN On the contrary. Even Gwalior could not break him. It is guardians of Islam like the honourable Sheikh who preserve the integrity of faith in this land where the infidels are in the majority.

DARA SHIKOH Your Honour, it is the openness of emperors like Akbar that has given Islam acceptance in the land and brought Muslim genius to the front. I could give you list upon list of the names of the buildings, paintings, poems and books produced because of this rich tradition. This, I believe, is the Mughal contribution to the world.

PROSECUTOR KHAN Even if we grant the Mughal achievements – and who can deny them, as they are all around us? – where is the link with Sufism, your brand of Islam?

DARA SHIKOH The connection between the idea of acceptance and openness that the mystics provide and the capacity of human beings to nurture their inner spiritual resources and artistic abilities is undisputed. Emperor Akbar is called the Mughal-e-Azam, 'the Great Mughal', because he created a strong and prosperous empire that harnessed the energies of all the faiths.

PROSECUTOR KHAN I still don't see the connection between Akbar, the Mughal-e-Azam, and Sufism.

DARA SHIKOH You are not looking too closely. Emperor Akbar's command to his governors was to spend their spare time reading Maulana Jalaluddin Rumi. Just imagine the power of the Mughal-e-Azam's directive. Instead of pastimes such as drinking and hunting, he directed his governors to read Rumi so that they could develop compassion in their hearts. Through compassion these rulers would be able to administer justice to ordinary people and the land would be content. Rumi, as you know, Your Honour, is the quintessential Sufi poet. That is the link between Emperor Akbar and Sufism: a link that eludes Abdullah Khan.

PROSECUTOR KHAN The defendant fails to mentions that the Emperor Akbar ruled through the might of his army, that after the Rajputs resisted him at Chittor he slaughtered thirty thousand people.

DARA SHIKOH True. But after that terrible bloodshed Emperor Akbar forever sought the path of peace and reconciliation, not unlike another great ruler of this land, Ashoka, after the bloody battle of Kalinga. Emperor Akbar's path is the true path.

PROSECUTOR KHAN That was all very well in the last century. This is a different time, a different age.

DARA SHIKOH Wrong again, Abdullah Khan. Our own beloved Emperor Shah Jehan is a great devotee of the celebrated Indian Sufi Sheikh Moin-uddin Chisti, who is buried in Ajmer. Indeed, for my own birth, Shah Jehan prayed like a humble supplicant at the shrine in Ajmer, and ordered celebrations throughout the empire when God heard his prayer.

PROSECUTOR KHAN And I am sure your miraculous birth, thanks to the Sufi saint, gave you special insights into the 'Great Secret'. And what a secret: prepare a dish with Hinduism and Islam, throw in Judaism and Christianity, and what do you have? Lo and behold, a dish we can all eat. What a great recipe, what a great secret. It is a dish calculated to give indigestion to anyone eating it.

QAZI FAIZUL HAQ Can we get to the closing arguments now? I believe the court has heard enough.

PROSECUTOR KHAN Yes. Yes, Your Honour. Let me sum up: Hindu mystics and yogis, Sikh gurus and dubious Sufis, these seem to define religion for Prince Dara. Note, Your Honour, the accused has not shown any remorse whatsoever during the proceedings. He remains unrepentant. He is adamant in his blasphemous, irresponsible and divisive beliefs. He is a danger to his own soul, and also to the future of the mighty Mughal Empire, the greatest empire in history; an empire that stretches from the mountains of Kabul in the north to the plains of the Deccan in the south, the deserts of Baluchistan in the west to the jungles of Burma in the east. I demand the maximum punishment for the crime of apostasy under Islamic law. I rest my case, Your Honour.

QAZI FAIZUL HAQ I think I have heard enough. As this court is based on the Islamic principles of justice, it is my duty to once again ask Prince Dara Shikoh if he would like to call any more witnesses before I decide the case.

PROSECUTOR KHAN Your Honour, I object. Who can be a more reliable witness than the accused himself? May I also remind Your Honour that the highest authority in the land is closely observing the proceedings of this case because of its nature, and justice must be swiftly done.

QAZI FAIZUL HAQ You do not have to remind the court of its duties, but I take your point.

PROSECUTOR KHAN I am so sorry, Your Honour, I do not mean to be –

QAZI FAIZUL HAQ In the name of God the Compassionate, the Merciful, let me sum up: Islamic jurisprudence demands swift and sure justice; there is no cause closer to God Almighty. Justice delayed is justice denied. I have taken notes and carefully heard the arguments presented for and against the accused. Having considered the arguments on both sides and examined the evidence in the light of the principles laid down in the holy Qur'an, I, Qazi Faizul Haq, find abundant evidence that the accused, Prince Dara Shikoh, is guilty of the crime of apostasy. The court therefore condemns him to be executed without delay.

A gasp goes up in the courtroom.

PROSECUTOR KHAN O Great Paragon of Justice, O Great –

QAZI FAIZUL HAQ Let me finish, please. Let this punishment be a lesson to others. God's justice embraces all, even members of the Imperial family. Such is the glory of the Mughal Empire.

COURT ATTENDEE 1 Mercy, o Judge! In the name of God, the Merciful, the Compassionate, show mercy!

COURT ATTENDEE 2 Spare our beloved prince; he is the people's prince!

COURT ATTENDEE 3 We will appeal to the Emperor for mercy!

COURT ATTENDEE 4 May Emperor Aurangzeb Alamgir reign for a thousand years!

QAZI FAIZUL HAQ Silence in the courtroom! According to the law of the land, the accused has twenty-four hours within which to appeal against the death sentence through a petition of mercy to be submitted to the Emperor. Even an apostate must be given this opportunity, as God is Compassionate and Merciful, and Islamic justice reflects these attributes of the Divine Being.

PROSECUTOR KHAN A Solomon, a wise judge, may God shower His blessings on you and your family, o Qazi Faizul Haq. History will remember you as having upheld the justice of the Emperor Jahangir; you have upheld the famed Adl-e-Jahangir of the Mughal Empire ...

Prosecutor Khan's words are drowned out by the voices of the courtroom attendees, who wail repeatedly.

COURT ATTENDEE 1 Mercy, show us mercy!

COURT ATTENDEE 2 We demand mercy!

QAZI FAIZUL HAQ The case is now closed. This court will adjourn.

Attendees continue to wail.

ACT II

SCENE ONE

Noon, the following day. Emperor Aurangzeb sits silently at centre-stage on a prayer mat. Attendant 2 stands unobtrusively behind him in a corner, arms folded and head bowed. The Emperor takes his time: he turns to the right; pauses; turns to the left; pauses; then holds up his palms in supplication. After a while, he makes a motion as though washing his face with his palms and slowly rises, speaking effortlessly, without even looking behind him.

AURANGZEB Ask her in.

Attendant 2 quietly disappears. Aurangzeb folds up the prayer mat and sits on a flat divan nearby that is covered with richly brocaded cloth with gold and crimson cushions. On a side-table are a roll of paper and an inkpot with a quill. Picking up his quill, Aurangzeb dips it in the ink and begins to slowly and carefully execute a Qur'anic verse in calligraphy.

ATTENDANT 2 (*returning and speaking in hushed tones*) Imperial Princess Jahanara is here.

JAHANARA (*entering*) Brother ...

AURANGZEB (*looking up*) *Assalaam alaikum*, sister.

JAHANARA *Wa alaikum assalaam*. You know, your calligraphed Qur'ans are collectors' items throughout the empire. Highly prized.

AURANGZEB (*continues to work, looking back down*) The better the sales, the more money I can give to charity. It is our Islamic duty. Now, what can I do for you, my sister?

JAHANARA Aurangzeb, I have been trying to see you since last night, but you are so difficult ...

AURANGZEB I am sorry, Jahanara, but I have been busy with affairs of state. We have the rumblings of a rebellion in the

Punjab again, and I am watching developments carefully. It is this new religion that is causing the trouble. I don't even understand their teachings. They seem to be neither Hindu nor Muslim, but have borrowed from both.

JAHANARA Yes, the Sikhs have created a marvellous synthesis of the great religions of India. Their community is one that promotes peace.

AURANGZEB Islam is the religion of peace. I don't see why a new way is required when we already have Islam.

JAHANARA The Sikhs walk the path of the Sufis. They are like spiritual brothers in a common quest for the Divine. After all, it was the celebrated Sufi saint Mian Mir who helped to lay the foundation of the Golden Temple.

AURANGZEB I can give you an Islamic response to challenge what you have just said, sister, but you have not come to discuss theology. Come sit by me, and tell me what I can do for you.

The Attendant 2 quietly arrives with glasses of sherbet and other delicacies, and places them in front of Aurangzeb and Jahanara.

JAHANARA Brother, I have come to plead for the life of Dara. I have the petition of mercy with me; please sign it and spare his life.

AURANGZEB (*puts away the quill and inkpot to give Jahanara his full attention*) I am sorry, sister; I cannot interfere with the judgment of the courts. I have appointed my finest Islamic scholars to run these courts, and we must allow justice to be done, and to be seen to done – especially when it concerns one of our own.

JAHANARA I am here to beg you for his life, in the name of Babur, the founder of the dynasty, in the name of Timur, from whom we derive our identity.

AURANGZEB Jahanara, you appear to be so agitated. This cannot be good for your health. Tell me, what has the court actually decided? I haven't yet seen the details.

JAHANARA (*handing Aurangzeb the mercy petition*) The *qazi* has condemned Dara to execution, but declared in court that the Emperor, in his wisdom, can sign a petition of mercy, and thereby save Dara's life.

AURANGZEB Hmm, let me look at this.

Aurangzeb takes the petition and places it on a pile of papers by the divan.

JAHANARA Please, brother, Dara has little time unless you intervene.

AURANGZEB Sister, please leave matters of state to me. I promise I will deal with this.

JAHANARA Dara has only 'til sunset, after which the orders of the *qazi* will be carried out.

AURANGZEB I have always respected you and looked up to you, Jahanara, even when you sided with our brother Dara. I have admired your goodwill for people, and your wisdom in most situations. You have great qualities of heart and head. I have even overlooked your infatuation with those heretical, so-called mystics, with their strange ways.

JAHANARA Brother, I am not here to discuss Sufism with you but to plead with you for my brother's life. If you truly respect me, you will do this for me. I implore you in the name of our beloved Prophet, who showed mercy even to his enemies who taunted him and wished to kill him. God is *Rahman* and *Rahmin*, Compassionate and Merciful; these are His greatest attributes; as a good Muslim, please show mercy, Aurangzeb.

AURANGZEB God is also the Just and the Avenger, and we must fear His wrath. He has chosen me to be the humble commander of the armies of Islam, and I will not allow anyone – anyone – to compromise my religious principles.

JAHANARA Think of our father, Aurangzeb.

AURANGZEB I do. I do. His wasteful ways and fanciful artistic expressions have left the treasury dangerously empty. I will not waste state money on grandiose building projects, just to satisfy my ego and end up bankrupting the empire. My focus will be to establish *madrassahs* and Islamic centres in order to strengthen the foundation of our faith.

JAHANARA Have a care. You are talking of a monument built by our father to honour our mother.

AURANGZEB That is why I made sure he could see it from his royal apartments in Agra until the end of his days.

JAHANARA I believe that is a cruel joke on our father. To imprison him in a place where he can barely glimpse the Taj Mahal from a slit in the wall, so he is reminded of the glory he once commanded and the plight of his present situation. Cruel indeed.

AURANGZEB I, too, shall create a monument that will outshine the so-called Taj Mahal, but it will be a mosque, and I will build it in Lahore to remind those rebellious Sikhs who rules this land. You will see that history will condemn our father for squandering public funds to create this monstrosity. It is doomed to be forgotten.

JAHANARA Even you, Aurangzeb, cannot deny the beauty, complexity and sophistication of the Taj. Do you know how many layers of symbolism exist around it?

AURANGZEB What I know is how much it cost; and I had heard

of a mad scheme for another Taj, this one made of black marble, to be built across the river Jamna.

JAHANARA Father planned to be buried in the black Taj, which would be an exact replica of the present one where Mother is buried.

AURANGZEB The extravagance takes my breath away. The treasury can barely sustain one Taj, and my father is dreaming of two.

JAHANARA For just one moment, Aurangzeb, set aside your doubts and scepticism. Let your imagination roam free. Think of our father's vision, of two Taj Mahals, one on either side of the river, connected by a delicate marble bridge. Think of the unity of that vision, its form and colour, one Taj representing sublimity, the other passion; one gentility, the other strength. Different worlds, yet connected. It is a breathtaking concept of unity, a spiritual expression of our very humanity. That is why everyone, rich or poor, Hindu or Sikh or Muslim, sees themselves in the Taj Mahal.

AURANGZEB The Mughal Empire rests in the sinews of our soldiers, not the dreams of our poets and artists.

JAHANARA Sometimes, it is hopeless to talk to you. I think you deliberately close your mind to me. But I hope you will open your heart to my request. I am here to persuade you to spare the life of our brother.

AURANGZEB Here, have some of this sweet delicacy, which I specially ordered for you, knowing that you would be visiting me. The English ambassador brought it from his land, and says it is made of a concoction of cocoa and milk. I know you are partial to it.

JAHANARA I confess my weakness for this delicacy; but I have no appetite today.

AURANGZEB Stop worrying, sister; I assure you justice will be done. I am here to ensure God's will is done. Now, I have matters of state to attend to. I shall call you in due course.

JAHANARA (*bows in salaam*) *Assalaam alaikum. Shab-e-khair.*

AURANGZEB Khuda hafiz.

Jahanara leaves quietly, in a dignified manner.

AURANGZEB (*quietly, as though to himself*) So, one sister begs for his life; I wonder what the other sister has to say?

Enter Roshanara, stepping out from behind the curtains hanging behind the divan.

ROSHANARA You see how dangerous he is. He has already sent a dagger to your heart by setting your naïve sister against you. And this trial has reduced the Mughal dynasty to a laughing-stock. People in the bazaar are recounting stories about the overzealous Abdullah Khan and how nobly Dara defended himself.

AURANGZEB Stories in the bazaar?

ROSHANARA Your favourite *qazi* had to insist on order several times. The trial has become a public spectacle, a *tamasha*, with all of Delhi talking about it. Dara remains popular with ordinary people.

AURANGZEB It seems these people have nothing better to do than to sit and gossip.

ROSHANARA Spare Dara and respect for our family along with its mystique will be lost forever. If he is allowed to continue, he will damage the Mughal Empire irreparably. There is already unrest among the Sikhs and Hindus, and they have the nerve to demand that Dara should be set free! They call him the rightful Emperor of India. They even complain that there would be no tax on them had Dara been the emperor. They demand that you back down from your path to impose Islam on India.

AURANGZEB Never. I will never abandon my duty to Islam. I will always quote the holy Prophet who, when he was pressured to give up Islam, said: 'I will never do so, even if you place the sun in the palm of one hand and the moon in the other.'

ROSHANARA That is what I admire in you, brother: your clear moral compass, especially in this dangerous time, when Islam needs strong leadership to unite and inspire people. They bless you and look to you as its champion.

AURANGZEB *Astaghfirallah*, only God is worthy of praise.

ROSHANARA I know you are modest, brother, but people still talk about the bandits and thieves whom you destroyed because they terrorised pilgrims on their way to the Haj. You tracked each and every one of them down, and punished them. You are seen as the true champion of Islam.

AURANGZEB My burden is heavy. How can I even put it in words? Sometimes I wonder whether I can carry the entire weight of my family, my dynasty and the future of Islam itself on my frail shoulders.

ROSHANARA No one apart from you can do so; that is why I admire you.

AURANGZEB You cannot imagine how much agony it gives me to have to pass harsh judgment after harsh judgment, even on my own blood.

ROSHANARA You must be steel. I truly believe, brother, you are all that stands between defeat and victory for Islam. You cannot fail. You must not fail.

AURANGZEB Sometimes, my sweet little sister, Roshan *Jan*, I feel so alone.

ROSHANARA I am always here, my brother.

AURANGZEB I feel like I carry the world on my shoulders.

ROSHANARA It is your destiny.

AURANGZEB (*glancing at the mercy petition*) So what do you think I should do with this?

ROSHANARA Sign it if you wish to destroy the Mughal Empire that your ancestors have nourished with their blood. Otherwise, do nothing. The Islamic court has already tried him and found him guilty of apostasy.

AURANGZEB Dara is our elder brother …

ROSHANARA Brother, never forget how close Dara came to capturing the throne. I don't have to remind you that he defeated the Imperial armies before you finally triumphed at Samugarh.

AURANGZEB I must admit that God was on our side that day, or we would have lost. Dara's son Sipihr led such bold charges, he almost broke through the left wing of my army; and Dara's Rajputs hammered on my right wing with such ferocity that I feared the battle would be lost. Then the miracle happened.

ROSHANARA What do you mean, brother?

AURANGZEB Quite unexpectedly a rocket hit the *howdah* in which Dara was sitting, and when he got off the elephant to mount a horse, his troops saw Dara's elephant without their leader. They feared he was dead and began to lose heart. I saw my chance and ordered my cavalry to charge Dara's centre, and thus smashed his army.

ROSHANARA Then, with a brilliant stroke, you took control of the Imperial treasury and ammunitions magazine at Agra.

AURANGZEB Yes, and prevented our father from further interfering on behalf of Dara. I had no choice but to order that our father be put under house arrest; but I allowed Jahanara to take care of him.

ROSHANARA So you agree that Dara came close to taking the throne.

AURANGZEB God is great.

ROSHANARA And if our loyal Afghan chieftain Malik Jiwan had not turned him over to us in Baluchistan, Dara might well have slipped across the border to the Persians. Who knows, then, perhaps he would have returned like our own ancestor, Emperor Humayun, with a Persian army to take Delhi.

AURANGZEB I was glad to finally capture Dara, but I cannot appreciate the actions of Malik Jiwan. He betrayed a guest, a member of the royal family at that, and one who had saved his miserable life when he stood condemned to die in court. This man has no honour whatsoever.

ROSHANARA Many would have done what Jiwan did. The very future of Islam in India is at stake, our destiny as Muslims in Hindustan. That is why so many nobles and generals and Islamic scholars are demanding that the *qazi*'s orders be implemented swiftly.

AURANGZEB You are right. I, too, have been thinking along these lines.

ROSHANARA Justice requires stern resolve and swift action.

AURANGZEB I know where you are going with this, but he *is* our elder brother. He is also extremely popular with people of all the faiths throughout the length and breadth of the empire. Even with the *firangi*. I know that Jahanara is in touch with them; they too demand that Dara's life be spared.

ROSHANARA She's too impressed by the *firangi*. Just see the silly pendant she wears around her neck all the time, with the picture of that strange, red-headed queen.

AURANGZEB The English ambassador took it off his own neck to give to her as a special gesture of appreciation.

ROSHANARA My elder sister has been too much in debt to the English ever since that accident. She believes that had it not been for the English doctor she would have never recovered from her burns.

AURANGZEB Well, Hakim Bukhari's balms and potions were of little use, and our father, typically, once again, showed his extravagance. Just imagine, giving the *firangi* a colony in Bengal! Jahanara's infatuation with them is annoying. They represent an obscure, tiny and powerless island off the coast of Europe. How dare they interfere with the Mughal Empire.

ROSHANARA Then deal with Dara swiftly. God has provided you with the opportunity. The Islamic court has found him guilty of apostasy. He will be forgotten after his death, and his message buried with him.

AURANGZEB *Ameen*. The sooner the better. Still, Roshan *Jan*, he is our elder brother. Perhaps exile ...

ROSHANARA No, brother, the stakes are too high, and you see how Dara can manipulate people. Just remember, it was he who poisoned the mind of your eldest daughter Zebunissa into believing the muddled nonsense that he preaches about mysticism. All your excellent teaching of orthodox Islam was lost on her. Can you imagine? Zebunissa now writes love poems.

AURANGZEB This is a matter of shame for me.

ROSHANARA She has given herself a pen name to disguise her identity and calls herself 'Makhfi', the Hidden One.

AURANGZEB To be fair to her, she has not supported Dara's naïve attempts to unite Islam and Hinduism. She draws the line in this regard.

ROSHANARA Of course. She is, after all, your daughter. But have you read her poetry? Its explicit passion would shock even the most hardened drunks in the most notorious taverns of Delhi.

AURANGZEB It breaks my heart to see Zebunissa in this condition. It is as though someone has done magic on her.

ROSHANARA She has no will in front of Dara, and thinks he is her master and inspiration. Dara manipulates her.

AURANGZEB (*to himself*) Zebu, my child ...

ROSHANARA What is most tragic is that a child who knew the Qur'an by heart when she was seven years old now writes love poetry of an explicit nature and wanders about in those bizarre black clothes. Who does she think she is, a mendicant Sufi or a Mughal princess, the daughter of the emperor himself? And Zebu's best friend is some Hindu girl who encourages her in everything she wants to do or say.

AURANGZEB Zebu's behaviour is a matter of shame.

ROSHANARA Dara must be stopped.

AURANGZEB (*rising without even looking at the mercy petition*) Sister, you must excuse me. I have to lead a military campaign.

ROSHANARA So you are returning to the Deccan.

AURANGZEB The Shi'i kingdoms are challenging the authority of Delhi. I have been diverted too long by this Dara business.

ROSHANARA Then you must close it before leaving Delhi. Too many illiterate fools believe that their Dara Shikoh, 'the Possessor of Glory', will bring them salvation.

AURANGZEB Enough, Roshanara, I have heard you. Keep me informed of the situation in Delhi.

Aurangzeb exits; Roshanara follows, a few feet behind.

SCENE TWO

The second day after the trial. A gloomy dungeon with straw on the floor and iron bars clearly visible to one side. On the straw sit Dara Shikoh and his son Sipihr. Both appear somewhat unkempt, dirty and desperate.

SIPIHR Father, I feel responsible for us being here, like this: prisoners waiting to die like common criminals.

DARA SHIKOH Sipihr *Jan*, you must never despair. Always trust in God. We have no idea why God does what He does. Maybe our death is our salvation. Maybe our defeat is the victory of our ideas.

SIPIHR No, Father, I wish I had fought better and harder at Samugarh. I was *this* close to breaking Uncle Aurangzeb's left wing, and our noble Rajput allies almost smashed his other wing. *This* close.

DARA SHIKOH It was written, my son. You were so heroic that day, and my heart was bursting with pride as I saw you in battle. You were truly named well: Sipihr, the sun. You scorched your enemies.

SIPIHR Yes, but the battle of Samugarh turned the tide against us.

DARA SHIKOH Let us not talk about defeat. I regret nothing in my life.

SIPIHR If only I had had more experience in battle; if only I had been a bit older, to give you more support.

DARA SHIKOH No, no, Sipihr *Jan*. Age has little to do with wisdom or courage. Your bravery was magnificent on the battlefield. You proved that you had the blood of Babur the Tiger in your veins. And do you know how old he was when he had to face his enemies, his own uncles? He was a mere boy, younger than you. And your other great hero, Akbar-e-Azam, he was also a boy when he ascended the throne of the Mughal Empire.

SIPIHR They are truly heroic figures, and I am so proud of them.

DARA SHIKOH But let us not talk of ancient history. I am truly sorry I could not spend more time with you. I would have liked to know you as a friend, Sipihr *Jan*.

SIPIHR You were doing such great things – changing the world. Single-handedly, you were altering the very image of Islam.

DARA SHIKOH Perhaps, my son; saving the world, and losing my family, those dearest to me. I wish I had spent more time with you. Now that we have this time together, I want to know you.

SIPIHR Why? Are we going to die? Will Uncle Aurangzeb have both of us killed? Surely his blood will prevent it.

DARA SHIKOH There is no point in deluding ourselves. Uncle Aurangzeb will do what he has to do. But son, I want to savour this time with you. Let us not waste it talking of Uncle Aurangzeb. Let us get to know each other.

SIPIHR What is the point, if we are doomed to die shortly?

DARA SHIKOH Time is a constraint in this mortal life alone. Our souls will live on. Go on, ask me any question that you may have wanted to ask.

SIPIHR Well, I – anything at all?

DARA SHIKOH Anything, my son.

SIPIHR Father, I must ask you a question that has been on my mind for some time; it is of a sensitive nature, but you have given me permission to ask any question.

DARA SHIKOH Of course, my son. What is it?

SIPIHR Hakim Bukhari and Aunt Roshanara have been speaking to me, chiding me. Auntie has been quite rude, really.

DARA SHIKOH About what, Sipihr?

SIPIHR She said you have wandered from the true path of Islam. She said that that is what the *ulema* were saying. She told me how dangerous this was, not only for the Mughal Empire but also for your soul.

DARA SHIKOH (*losing his temper*) This is nonsense, Sipihr! This Roshanara remains a narrow-minded parrot of her brother's ideas.

SIPIHR But she said there was a danger to your soul, and I love you so much, Father.

DARA SHIKOH I don't have to explain my faith to anyone. Islam teaches me that only God will judge us. I know how much I love the Prophet of Islam, peace be upon him, how much he inspires me. My task has been to share his vision of compassion and humanity with everyone.

SIPIHR But the *ulema* don't see this. Aunt Roshanara says –

DARA SHIKOH Maybe I have made a mistake. I should have made allowances for the feelings of the *ulema*. Perhaps I have been too provocative for them. It might have been wrong of me to goad them so much. I should have resisted the temptation. But I did enjoy seeing them becoming mad with rage; and they claim to speak on behalf of God's compassion.

SIPIHR That is exactly what I told Aunt Roshanara.

DARA SHIKOH Yes, I will try harder with our learned *ulema* in the future. They constantly misunderstand my position. I wish to open the doors of Islam to everyone. The *ulema* wish to close Islam's doors. I wish to convey the beauty of its message to everyone. Besides, we live in a world with so many other wonderful faiths, and we must live in peace and harmony or we end up destroying the very foundations of faith itself.

SIPIHR What surprises me is that Uncle Aurangzeb does not appreciate what you are doing. He is such a champion of Islam. I would have thought ...

DARA SHIKOH I would have thought so too, but Aurangzeb is a complicated man.

SIPIHR Tell me, Father, about my Uncle Aurangzeb. What was he like as a young man?

DARA SHIKOH I thought we were not going to talk of him.

SIPIHR Your insights will help me understand what is happening to us better.

DARA SHIKOH Aurangzeb was quite normal as a young man.

SIPIHR I heard he was without fear.

DARA SHIKOH That he was. Once an enraged elephant charged at Emperor Shah Jehan, and Aurangzeb galloped in front of it to stop it from attacking. Aurangzeb was thrown off his horse, but stood his ground until other horsemen arrived to subdue the beast.

SIPIHR Uncle Aurangzeb has a reputation as a successful military commander, as a man of the sword.

DARA SHIKOH The sword, my son, is always a double-edged weapon, and injures both he who wields it and he who is attacked.

SIPIHR What do you mean?

DARA SHIKOH One day you will find out.

SIPIHR Strange are the ways of God, that this brave and noble prince became such a stern, unsmiling man. Have you heard the story of Uncle Aurangzeb and the musicians?

DARA SHIKOH Which one? There are so many.

SIPIHR The musicians of Delhi were ordered to put away their instruments by Uncle Aurangzeb, as he did not wish to promote music. They held a mock funeral procession with a shrouded 'corpse' made up of musical instruments. Uncle Aurangzeb, hearing their wailing, asked them who was dead, and whom they were burying. 'Music,' they answered. 'Bury it deep, then,' said Uncle Aurangzeb, 'so that it does not rise again.'

DARA SHIKOH (*smiling*) Yes, I have heard this story.

SIPIHR Was he always so loveless? Do you recall Uncle Aurangzeb ever with ordinary emotions, like the rest of us? Was he ever in love?

DARA SHIKOH You will be surprised: he was. In fact, he was so much in love that when his beloved died, something seemed to die in him.

SIPIHR Uncle Aurangzeb in love? Wonders will never cease. Who was she?

DARA SHIKOH You will be even more surprised to hear who she was: a Hindu dancing girl. Yes, a Hindu girl had won the heart of your Uncle Aurangzeb, the champion of Islam.

SIPIHR Truly, wonders will never cease.

DARA SHIKOH That is why poets say: the ways of love are mysterious.

SIPIHR Well, Father, I have always wondered what it would be like to fall in love.

DARA SHIKOH Sipihr, you are barely fifteen years old. You will find out.

SIPIHR To be truly, passionately in love, to find the true soulmate, to belong in body and soul to someone else.

DARA SHIKOH (*smiling*) You speak like a young man who reads much about love but has still to experience it.

SIPIHR Tell me, Father, I mean, can I ask you ... *any* question?

DARA SHIKOH Of course. I gave you permission.

SIPIHR Have you – have you ever been in love?

DARA SHIKOH The question of a young man, and not entirely unexpected; after all, we are speaking as friends.

SIPIHR Tell me, then, Father. I would really like to know.

DARA SHIKOH Yes, my son, I have loved.

SIPIHR I mean deeply and madly in love.

DARA SHIKOH Yes.

SIPIHR I don't mean your mystical or Sufi kind of love.

DARA SHIKOH Hm, well ...

SIPIHR Please, Father, I would really like to know.

DARA SHIKOH I would say it was Ranadil.

SIPIHR Nek Bibi *Jan*?

DARA SHIKOH Yes.

SIPIHR I can't picture her in any way but covered in shawls and veils and fasting and praying.

DARA SHIKOH She wasn't always like that. She wasn't always my wife. You know, I first heard of her when I was a young man. It seemed everyone in North India was in love with her, and sang her praises: this bewitching dancing girl from the Punjab.

SIPIHR Did her being a Hindu matter to anyone when you wished to marry her?

DARA SHIKOH Yes, it did; certainly to the orthodox and narrow-minded.

SIPIHR How could Hinduism be a problem when my grandfather Emperor Shah Jehan was the son of a Hindu himself?

DARA SHIKOH Perhaps that is why he did not want his sons to marry Hindus.

SIPIHR Would you mind if I asked you what it felt like?

DARA SHIKOH What it felt like?

SIPIHR When you first met her and fell in love.

DARA SHIKOH Well, son, you will find out one day.

SIPIHR Tell me, Father, tell me.

DARA SHIKOH It was like intoxication; like being completely drunk every minute of every hour, every day.

SIPIHR Like your passion for the Divine?

DARA SHIKOH In a way, yes. Love is the purest expression of devotion. It is only through love that your soul really begins to explore its own capacity to reach towards the mysteries of creation.

SIPIHR Yes, but tell me more about your human emotions. What, for instance, did you love best about Nek Bibi *Jan*?

DARA SHIKOH Well, there were so many things about her that I loved. Her laughter; she made me laugh. Her eyes; I loved those dark and mysterious windows to the universe itself.

SIPIHR Father, you sound like a poet in love.

DARA SHIKOH Love makes everyone a poet, my son.

SIPIHR Did you ever write any love poems to Nek Bibi *Jan*?

DARA SHIKOH My poems express my love for God.

SIPIHR I am never sure, when your verses talk about 'the Beloved', whether they mean God or some woman.

DARA SHIKOH A woman's verses could suggest they are addressed to a man. A good example is the poetry of your cousin Zebunissa, and her references to the Beloved. It's a deliberate ambiguity that mystics create in order to throw the orthodox off the scent. But when they write of the Beloved, they mean God.

SIPIHR Was my cousin Zebunissa any good?

DARA SHIKOH Yes, she was my favourite pupil and wrote beautiful verses. One of my favourite poems is something she called *I bow before the image of my Love.*

SIPIHR How does it go? Do you remember any lines?

DARA SHIKOH Let me see ... I used to remember some lines that struck me as particularly moving:

No Muslim I, but an idolater
I bow before the image of my Love
and worship Her.
No Brahman I
my sacred thread
I cast away, for round my neck I wear
Her plaited hair instead.

SIPIHR By God, that is so bold. I never suspected my quiet, sweet cousin would have such passion lurking in her. I look forward to really getting to know her, when I am out of this place.

DARA SHIKOH I remember some more lines from another poem of hers that left an impression on me:

Here is the path of love – how dark and long
its winding ways, with many snares beset!
Yet crowds of eager pilgrims onward throng
and fall like doves into the fowler's net …
But Makhfi, tell me where the feast is made,
where are the merry-makers? Lo, apart
here in my soul the feast of God is laid,
within the hidden chambers of my heart.

SIPIHR It is very profound. Very Sufi. So she called herself 'Makhfi'. No wonder Uncle Aurangzeb was mad at her.

DARA SHIKOH Yes, it's a pity your uncle doesn't appreciate poetry or literature.

SIPIHR Nor music, nor anything artistic or creative. It's a miracle that poor Zebu has survived so long with a father like that.

DARA SHIKOH Her poems cost her the love of her father. You know, she was his favourite child, and he particularly wished to groom her to follow in his orthodox learning of Islam.

SIPIHR What was the story of Zebunissa writing a line of verse that infuriated her father?

DARA SHIKOH That was typical of my brother. He had grown weary of his daughter's poetic fame and arranged for a famous poet to challenge her in a poetry contest. The poet would recite the first line of a verse, and Zebu would have to complete it in rhyme while matching the subject. If she failed to do so within three days, Aurangzeb declared, she would have to renounce poetry forever.

SIPIHR That was harsh. What was the first line?

DARA SHIKOH 'Rare it is to find a black and white pearl ...'

SIPIHR 'Rare it is to find a black and white pearl.' What does that mean? What happened then?

DARA SHIKOH Zebu felt crushed after three days, as she could not find the answer; in desperation she prepared to take her own life by swallowing her diamond ring. At this point her best friend began to cry profusely. Seeing her friend's tears, Zebu began to smile, and then clapped her hands in joy and laughed loudly.

SIPIHR I don't understand, Father.

DARA SHIKOH Zebu had found the answer in the tears of her friend. This friend had big, beautiful eyes, and she lined them with *kohl* or *surma*. Zebu saw the dark *surma* run from her friend's eyes as she cried, forming little black and white 'pearls'. So as the first verse was 'Rare it is to find a black and white pearl', Zebu's next line was: 'Except the *surma*-mingled tear of a beauty.'

SIPIHR What an amazing story. I am sure Uncle would have been furious.

DARA SHIKOH Zebu summoned him, and Aurangzeb came running, because he thought he had triumphed and would now finally silence Zebunissa's poetry.

A guard approaches, and stops outside the cell.

GUARD O Prince. I bring an Imperial order.

SIPIHR Father, he has news for us! Uncle Aurangzeb has reprieved us!

The guard bows his head but does not reply to this.

DARA SHIKOH Speak.

GUARD I am ashamed, o Noble Prince ...

DARA SHIKOH Please, do your duty.

GUARD I have been asked to convey the orders of execution

to the prisoner, Prince Dara Shikoh. The prisoner must make himself ready at daybreak, at the time of the morning prayer, for the implementation of the orders of the *qazi*'s court.

DARA SHIKOH I will be ready, *insh'allah*.

SIPIHR Father, what does this mean? Is there no justice, no compassion in this land?

Sipihr wobbles, suddenly weak in the knees. Dara Shikoh puts his arms around his son.

DARA SHIKOH Have faith, Sipihr *Jan*, have faith. We must never fear the sword. The Beloved is with us here in this very room, and awaits us outside it.

GUARD I take my leave, Noble Prince.

DARA SHIKOH (*goes up to the cell door*) Yes, but wait. What happens to Prince Sipihr? Is he free to go?

GUARD It has been ordered that he be taken to another prison, where he will spend the rest of his days.

DARA SHIKOH The rest of his days ... Where, which prison?

GUARD Gwalior Fort.

DARA SHIKOH (*slowly collapsing to the ground*) No, not Gwalior Fort.

SIPIHR (*puts his arms around Dara Shikoh*) Father, we must not despair. You have taught me that.

ACT III

Evening, September 1681 – twenty-two years since Dara Shikoh's execution. The balcony of the famous Red Fort in Delhi, overlooking the Jamna River. A light breeze touches the muslin curtains. In the distance we hear Indian classical music. Jahanara reclines on a divan, gravely ill. She has a faraway expression on her face. Jahanara's attendant fusses over her. Enter Aurangzeb, accompanied by Imperial Chief Physician Hakim Bukhari. Aurangzeb has aged visibly, with a white beard and a stoop. He and Hakim Bukhari pause and speak out of range of Jahanara.

HAKIM BUKHARI Everything possible is being done, Your Majesty.

AURANGZEB She has been so weak these past few days. Her mind is wandering. I fear the worst ...

HAKIM BUKHARI God will be merciful.

AURANGZEB I have entrusted my sister's health to you as a physician. So please leave God out of this.

HAKIM BUKHARI I am sorry, Your Majesty, I meant –

AURANGZEB Have you talked to the *firangi* physician yet?

HAKIM BUKHARI Dr Smith was away from Delhi, but is returning at my request. I will be seeing him as soon as he comes back.

AURANGZEB See that everything is done to ensure the comfort of Her Imperial Highness.

HAKIM BUKHARI Of course, Your Majesty.

With the faintest gesture, Aurangzeb motions for Hakim Bukhari to leave. Hakim Bukhari exits, head bowed, hands folded, careful that his back is never turned towards the Emperor. Aurangzeb stands quietly, watching Jahanara for a while.

AURANGZEB (*slowly moving towards Jahanara*) And how is my beloved sister feeling this morning?

JAHANARA (*motionless, speaking slowly*) Who is that?

Aurangzeb motions to Jahanara's attendant to leave. She moves quickly, head bowed, always facing Aurangzeb so as not to turn her back on him.

AURANGZEB Jahanara, it is I, your beloved brother, Aurangzeb.

JAHANARA (*attempts to sit up*) I don't feel so well today.

AURANGZEB The English doctor will see you shortly, and I promise you, you'll feel better. I hope Bukhari has been taking care of you in the meantime?

JAHANARA How are you, brother?

AURANGZEB I am as well as can be, sister. The problems of state demand all my time and energy.

JAHANARA You look tired.

AURANGZEB I don't get rest. There are unending challenges to Muslim rule in India. The Sikhs have revolted in the Punjab, the Hindus in Central India; and that Sivaji has become a thorn in my side. The Mahrattas have found a dangerous leader.

JAHANARA You must take special care of your Hindu and Sikh subjects.

AURANGZEB But I do. There is propaganda against me, that I am a fanatic. Don't they know that my top generals are Hindus? That I have sanctioned lands and grants to Hindu temples? That I have –

JAHANARA Even your Muslim subjects ... The Pathans in the north are unhappy, the Shi'is in the south ...

AURANGZEB This has to do with the sheer size of India. The Empire has never had so great a reach. Mughal armies now command the largest territory in history.

JAHANARA The ordinary man is not concerned with the grandeur and glory of the Empire.

AURANGZEB I work night and day for Islam. To unify the land, I have established Islamic schools and codified Islamic law.

JAHANARA People need something more than law.

AURANGZEB More than law? What can that be?

JAHANARA Love. The path of Dara ...

AURANGZEB Dara? What made you think of him?

JAHANARA Sometimes at dusk I hear his voice. He calls to me. He speaks of love and compassion.

AURANGZEB Do not begin to speak of such things, Jahanara. Nothing is to be gained from it.

JAHANARA (*becomes increasingly agitated while speaking, and is sitting up by the time she has finished*) On moonlit nights, I find myself on Shah Jehan's magical bridge. I look down at the magnificent Jamna, and it sparkles and glitters. I see tiny golden fairies with silver wings diving into the dark waters and coming up with sapphires and emeralds and rubies in their hands. I dream of a world at peace with itself. At the centre of the bridge I see a small gathering of sages from every religion and of every colour. In the midst of this group I see a golden glow, and underneath it sits Prince Dara Shikoh.

AURANGZEB (*gently, moving to her*) Jahanara, please. You must not agitate yourself.

JAHANARA I hear laughter and music. Friends talking and reciting poetry.

AURANGZEB Those were frivolous gatherings. They encouraged un-Islamic thoughts and behaviour.

JAHANARA *What shall I do?*

I know not what I am
I am not a Christian

I am neither Jew
nor Gabonese, nor a Muslim.

AURANGZEB (*softly, shaking his head in disapproval*) Blasphemy.

JAHANARA (*with tears in her eyes*)

I am neither of the East
nor of the West
Neither of the Earth, nor the ocean
Only Him, I search, only Him, I know
Only Him, I see, and only Him, I call
He is the beginning and the end.

AURANGZEB This is blasphemy, Jahanara.

JAHANARA Then execute me, like you executed the writer of these verses.

AURANGZEB This invocation of Dara is morbid. He was threatening Islam; I had to –

JAHANARA (*increasingly agitated*) Why were you so cruel? Why, Aurangzeb?

AURANGZEB That was a different time. I did what I thought was right. For Islam. For the future of the Mughal Empire.

JAHANARA To humiliate him, the most noble prince of the Mughal dynasty ... To parade him and Sipihr on a dirty, mangy, female elephant; to send his head in a box to our father. To kill Sipihr, a mere boy, innocent and brave!

AURANGZEB Sister, don't think of the past. Many mistakes were made. But let us not talk about these matters, as no purpose is served.

JAHANARA The weeks after Dara's death were the worst of my life. I felt my better half had been killed. We were one soul in two bodies. People were right when they said that.

AURANGZEB Please, Jahanara.

JAHANARA But my loss was nothing compared to the grief of our father. I still hear that long, slow, haunting groan from the depths of his soul when he saw Dara's head. The once mighty Emperor collapsed in agony. I thought he would never forgive you.

AURANGZEB Yet you persuaded him to forgive me. He forgave me on his deathbed in his magnanimity, even as he lay dying. I regret that my advisers –

JAHANARA You have always had bad advisers. Sycophants. Time-servers.

AURANGZEB There I will agree with you.

JAHANARA Even the title they gave you: *Alamgir.* 'World Conqueror.' 'Owner of the Universe.'

AURANGZEB Yes, I now realise some of these things. They even convinced me that the Mughal Empire was at the centre of the world; that the kings of England and France were like our petty chieftains.

JAHANARA They persuaded you to do away with my beloved brother Dara. Why did you allow it? Why?

AURANGZEB Sister, stop harking back to the past. It will do us no good. I had to – and have to – defend Islam.

JAHANARA You know it had nothing to do with Islam.

AURANGZEB What do you mean?

JAHANARA Jealousy. Plain and simple.

AURANGZEB Jealousy?

JAHANARA You were jealous of Dara.

AURANGZEB I? Aurangzeb. Jealous of Dara. How can you say that?

JAHANARA He was loved by everyone. And you went after all of

Dara's favourites with a vengeance. Even poor Sarmad, a harmless mystic. It was the same with Dara's beloved, Ranadil.

AURANGZEB I did offer her marriage after Dara's death, so that I could preserve her status and give her security. Dara's other wife agreed.

JAHANARA Ranadil preferred to slash her face with a blade.

AURANGZEB These women make no sense to me.

JAHANARA What integrity. What beauty. All sacrificed for her beloved Dara.

AURANGZEB She had a duty to her emperor.

JAHANARA An ordinary dancing girl had shown the Emperor of India the meaning of love. This Hindu girl from Lahore has entered the realm of legend in the Mughal annals of Hindustan.

AURANGZEB I didn't see it in that way.

JAHANARA You didn't even spare your own daughter, Zebunissa.

AURANGZEB She was just a child, but Dara filled her mind with dangerous thoughts.

JAHANARA You imprisoned that hapless princess for life. You silenced the rare beauty of her mystic verses.

AURANGZEB The enemies of Islam were exploiting her, using her to undermine Islam.

JAHANARA Nothing but jealousy.

AURANGZEB Nonsense. For me, sister, matters of state must take precedence over everything. I must look to the future.

JAHANARA I fear for the future, brother.

AURANGZEB Only God can tell the future. We can but do our best in the light of His instructions.

The aazan, *the Muslim call to prayer, floats into the room.*

AAZAN (O.S.) God is Great ... God is Great ... Come to Prayer ... Come to Prayer ... Come to what is good for you ... Come to what is good for you ...

AURANGZEB I must go to offer my prayers.

JAHANARA I miss him every day and every hour.

AURANGZEB I will return tomorrow to check how you are feeling. You must rest now.

JAHANARA (*sighs softly*) I will, brother. The time is near when we will meet again.

AURANGZEB Please, Princess. You must not exhaust yourself. You are most dear to us.

JAHANARA You honour me. You have always been kind to me.

AURANGZEB It is my duty. Now rest.

JAHANARA I shall rest. I shall rest peacefully in the courtyard of the renowned Nizamuddin Aulia, in the company of Amir Khusro, the legendary mystic poet.

AURANGZEB Your wishes will be honoured, I promise. When the time comes, you will be buried in the presence of the Saint of Delhi.

JAHANARA Ideal company for eternity. Surrounded by saints, poets and seekers ... And you ...? Still planning a simple, unmarked, anonymous grave? A true Muslim to the end.

AURANGZEB God alone is worthy of praise. I haven't changed my mind about how I wish to be buried. But enough talk of death, sister. India needs you. I need you, Jahanara.

I need your love and your advice, more than ever. No one speaks to me with your candour and integrity.

JAHANARA I am tired ... (*closes her eyes and reclines back into the divan*). *Shab-e-khair.* I want to sleep.

Aurangzeb leans forward and kisses her on the forehead.

AURANGZEB (*speaking softly, as though to himself*) *Khuda Hafiz.* God be with you. You are a true saint. I know you will intercede for me with Dara. May God have mercy on our souls.

Aurangzeb quietly exits the room.

Lights fade.